The Librarian's Guide to Genealogical Research

James Swan

Highsmith Press Handbook Series

Highsmith PRESS

Fort Atkinson, Wisconsin

Published by Highsmith Press LLC
W5527 Highway 106
P.O. Box 800
Fort Atkinson, Wisconsin 53538-0800
1-800-558-2110

The paper used in this publication meets the minimum requirements of
American National Standard for Information Science —
Permanence of Paper for Printed Library Material. ANSI/NISO Z39.48-1984.

Some material in this publication is reprinted by permission of The Church of Jesus Christ of Latter-
day Saints. In granting permission for this use of copyright material, the Church does not imply or
express either endorsement or authorization of this publication.
Family History Library™ is a trademark of The Church of Jesus Christ of Latter-day Saints.
Ancestral File™ is a trademark of The Church of Jesus Christ of Latter-day Saints.
Family History Library Catalog™ is a trademark of The Church of Jesus Christ of Latter-day Saints.
International Genealogical Index® is a registered trademark of The Church of Jesus Christ of
    Latter-day Saints.

Library of Congress Cataloging-in-Publication Data
Swan, James.
        The librarian's guide to genealogical research / James Swan.
            p.   cm. -- (Highsmith Press handbook series)
        Includes bibliographical references and index.
        ISBN 0-57950-011-0   (alk. paper)
        1. Genealogical libraries--United States. I. Title. II. Series.
        Z675.G44S93 1998
929' .1' 072073--dc21   98-26997
                                                        CIP

Contents

WITHDRAWN

Introduction

The Librarian's Guide to Genealogical Research is both a readable introduction and a reference book. It's designed to help you understand the processes and tools available for family history research, design a reference service in your library, and navigate your way through the sea of resources for family historians on the Internet and from other libraries. Special focus is given to strengthening local library collections and to identifying the best tools and sources for finding information beyond your local community.

As you begin reading *The Guide*, it will be helpful to think of providing genealogical research as a process. It's also important to understand that helping people find their ancestors can be very challenging for any librarian—but it doesn't have to be overwhelming. Any interested librarian can learn to be proficient at answering genealogical research questions, and can successfully develop a strong genealogical collection, no matter how large or small it might be.

One of the best starting points in providing genealogical reference service is to do some work on your own family tree. With this in mind, the first three chapters of *The Guide* have been designed as a basic primer on family history research and sources. You may choose to take the book home and use it to get started on your own genealogy—from which you will gain valuable insights into the excitement and challenges your patrons face when they bring their research to the library. These same chapters will be useful to help your patrons with their research. Many will find the charts, checklists and forms helpful. Others will benefit from the explanations of the various tools we will discuss.

Later chapters serve as information links to the best and largest genealogical resources available in libraries and archives throughout the United States. I have tried whenever possible to include helpful information you can use right away to access other libraries or answer research questions. For example, instead of simply telling you about Cyndi Howells' Web site, with an overwhelming 30,000+ genealogy links, I have annotated a much shorter list of significant Web sites that you will want to review. I have viewed all of the resources selected for *The Guide* in this way, essentially as "first link" sources—agencies, organizations, libraries and tools that it's important to know about and to know how to access.

A Training Manual

The Librarian's Guide to Genealogical Research can also serve as a training manual for support staff or volunteers. Sometimes genealogical reference questions are difficult to answer because the researcher needs more specific answers than we are used to providing at the reference desk. The explanations here give an overview of what information can be found in various types of documents. And a caution—you can't expect it to all become clear at once. Patience and dedication are the virtues most needed by librarians who serve genealogists. It takes time and patience to learn about genealogists' information needs, and it takes dedication to develop the resources in your library to help them. It's also important to know when to say, "We don't have that information in our library. You need to try the courthouse or the Family History Center."

When I first started *The Librarian's Guide to Genealogical Research*, I didn't realize how little was available to help librarians help genealogists. There are many books and other resources for researchers, but very little targeted for the specific needs of librarians. This book may not tell you everything you need to know about serving the needs of genealogical researchers, but it will help you sort through what is out there.

Scope

I have included both the obvious and the obscure in this book. There is information that will help you connect your patrons with the resources of the well-known Family History Library® in Salt Lake City, and you will also be introduced to a much less known, but neat little newsletter called *Life Stories* that can help family historians write their family's story. I have tried to get to the essence of each source and resource without letting a lot of extraneous stuff get in the way. At the same time, I have included enough detail so you won't have to go to another source to find out how to move on the suggestion I have presented.

Because this is a concise guide, I have decided to limit the scope to the United States. I know we all have roots that lead to another country if we go back far enough. To get you started in this area, I have included a few ethnic resources, and they will take you to many other foreign resources. I mention libraries and other research facilities in almost every state, but I have not included bibliographic references to tools that limit themselves to a single state or a particular county. I considered these resources as "second or third link" tools. They are referenced repeatedly in the tools I do mention.

My Experience Serving Genealogists

For me, learning genealogical reference service was a sink-or-swim experience. The year I was a junior in college I worked on the fourth floor of the Brigham Young University library. I was the reference librarian on Saturdays and evenings. The fourth floor of the BYU library houses the history and genealogical collection. I had taken a genealogy class when I was a sophomore and a library science general reference class—hardly the preparation necessary to answer the type of questions I was going to get on the fourth floor; but I survived. Like other opportunities in life, when my enthusiasm outweighed my knowledge, I jumped in with both feet and learned the collection. I also began in earnest doing my own genealogy. As I started researching my own family tree I learned what was in the collection. I helped compile a bibliography of genealogical sources available in the BYU library. Eventually, I was able to really help an increasing number of the people.

An Overview

I believe genealogical research must begin with the reference interview, just like any other reference search. Sometimes you may have to ask several questions to find out the real information need. Once you have identified that first specific question, the best thing you can do is help the patron get the answer to that question. Working with the tools you have in your collection, you will want to connect them with the book, film, or CD that has the best chance of containing the information they want.

A Review of the Sources

No library is going to have every genealogical tool in the world, but all can have the sources that are most significant to their local communities and additional resources that support research beyond the community. To develop the collection best suited for their own community, librarians need to know what types of records are available, what kinds of information they contain and where to find them. In Chapter 1, we will take a look at lots of resources and the best places to find them. I even suggest first places to look for some of the essential facts genealogists are always seeking. It is entirely reasonable to expect that resources of genealogical value, especially local information, will be found in the smallest of small libraries.

Robin Dombrowsky, of the Leesburg (Florida) Public Library had this to say about the resources of small libraries: "The largest collection is not necessarily the best for all people. I have had individuals quite irritated that they had spent a lot of money and time going to Allen County and couldn't find anything they needed.

"The best library may be a small town library with a couple of shelves of genealogical material if it is on your family. In my own personal research, I found a history of the church my grandmother and her family attended in St. Joseph, Michigan, in Tarpon Springs, which is not the first place I'd go. It contained a list of confirmands which included her as well as her brothers, sisters and in-laws. It even had photos of some of the classes. I considered that a real find."

Even the smallest libraries should have copies of local newspapers, cemetery books, and local histories. Other resources are more logically found in the county courthouse or a local funeral home. It is also reasonable to expect individuals or family members will have some of the most valuable pieces of family history in their homes. Chapter 1 has a checklist of these kinds of sources to assist researchers trying to collect all the personal sources available to them.

The Genealogical Research Process

A clear understanding of the research process is essential to providing quality reference service to family historians. Identifying a particular ancestor and searching for information about him or her, evaluating and recording the information, and then selecting another ancestor and applying the same procedure is how the process works. The cyclical nature of genealogical research lends itself to many opportunities to teach it and explain it to patrons. Locating the documents that have the information the patrons want is the job of the reference librarian regardless of the subject. In chapter 2 we will present some ideas and resources to help you develop your genealogical reference skills.

Recently, I was helping a patron who wanted to know more about his uncle who had died in a automobile accident in 1945. He had a name and the town. We found the individual in the Barton County Cemetery book with "1927– 1945" as his dates. He needed a more exact death date to find an obituary, so I called the funeral home in the town where the uncle had lived. They had the burial date, and the patron was able to find the obituary in the newspaper we have on microfilm.

It would have been a waste if time to suggest searching the *Ancestral File* ® (which we have in our library) to this researcher. To suggest that step to another patron might have been entirely consistent with good reference service. Chapter 2 provides a framework for making these decisions.

Using Gathered Data

Since genealogical research is a quest, a hobby, or perhaps just a lifelong pursuit, genealogists have recurring and evolving information needs. The next objective is to help patrons evaluate the data they've collected and offer suggestions that go beyond the scope of the question that brought them into the library. In chapter 3 we will review getting organized and how to help novices use forms to save their work. Not all suggestions will be appropriate in all situations, and this chapter will give you the tools for assessing what kind of help patrons may need next.

Collection Development

Having identified the wide range of places where genealogical information might be found in chapter 1, in chapter 4 I focus on collection development in your local library. These tools for the library collection will be "next link" resources for genealogists. The how-to-books will help genealogists conduct their research, evaluate their findings, organize the information and record it. The directories will help them find other organizations that can provide the information they are seeking. The section on guidebooks will tell you where to look for more detailed information from important sources. The catalogs will make you aware of places to find additional materials for your library. Most importantly, we provide you with a checklist of the local resources you will want to make sure your library has.

Other Agencies

In chapters 5 and 6 we discuss other libraries and agencies that have materials of value for genealogists. In doing the research for *The Guide*, I conducted a survey of libraries and archives to gather more information about their services to genealogists. From the responses, I created a list focussed reference service, collection size, electronic access, and ILL. In other words, to make it on my list the organization had to do more than just open its doors and say, "Here we are folks. Come to us and use our genealogical materials." The list is fairly long and gives you enough facts about each organization to help your patrons decide if they want to contact the institution or go there for more information. Some facilities like the Family History Library in Salt Lake City and the National Archives deserve special attention. For the exceptional institutions, I created a Top 10 list. These are major resource centers where researchers spend lots of time and novices can get lost without a map. For these, I have included tips on how to benefit most from a trip to a major research facility.

The list here is the biggest and the best. There are many, many other libraries that have materials of great value to genealogists. One place to look for a more comprehensive listing of libraries and archives is *The Genealogist's Address Book* by Elizabeth Petty Bentley listed in chapter 4. It has many names, addresses, and telephone numbers, and every library should have a copy. Also, each year the May/June issue of *Everton's Genealogical Helper* has a "Directory of Genealogical Libraries."

Computers and Genealogy

Although I will say it many times in the book, there is no way I can overemphasize the effect that computers had on the way we do genealogical research. In chapters 7 and 8, we will discuss their potential for use by individuals and in the library. Genealogical software for personal computers has changed the way genealogists organize and record data. The GEDCOM protocol has revolutionized and streamlined the way we share data. The Internet and email have dramatically increased the speed of communication between researchers and the way they share information.

Hiring a Professional

In life we try to do a lot of things on our own. We fix our plumbing problems and our cars. We even do our own income tax returns, but when the task seems more than we can handle on our own, we turn to a professional. We hire someone to do it for us. Searching for our ancestors can be the same way—especially if our research leads us to sources we cannot read because they are in a different language. In chapter 9, we will discuss the issue of hiring a professional researcher and how to assure the best results.

Why Do People Undertake Genealogical Research?

For the family historians that enter your library, family history may be a compelling interest or a hobby or may be pursued for religious reasons. People may have heard that they were related to someone famous and want to find out if it is true. Other people just feel drawn to find their ancestors and they can't explain why. They get excited when they find information that will take them back another generation.

One of the most significant sources for family history researchers is the Family History Library in Salt Lake City, which contains the collections on family history of The Church of Jesus Christ of Latter-day Saints. The Church has committed millions of dollars to help members around the world find their ancestors. The vast resources of the Family History Library® and its worldwide network of Family History Centers® are part of the plan to make it easier for everyone to trace their family trees. Since these facilities are open to the public, it behooves librarians to become acquainted with their services. A brief explanation of the importance of family history research to LDS members is helpful in appreciating the commitment of resources the Church has made.

The Church of Jesus Christ of Latter-day Saints

Every year hundreds of thousands of Latter-day Saints (LDS), an abbreviation for members of The Church of Jesus Christ of Latter-day Saints, visit one of the 60+ temples around the world to do vicarious ordinance work for their dead ancestors. Latter-day Saints believe that certain earthly ordinances like baptism and confirmation are necessary for salvation. They also believe in sealing spouses together and sealing children to parents in eternal families. These vicarious ordinances are performed by the living for, and on behalf of the dead. LDS Temples are the only church buildings where these ordinances are performed. On the other side of the veil, the spirits of those for whom the work has been performed will have the opportunity to accept or reject the work that has been done for them. Before any ordinance work can be done in LDS Temples, individuals must be accurately identified and linked in marriages and family relationships. Latter-day Saints compile their genealogies so that temple ordinances can be performed for their ancestors.

I am a genealogist as well as a librarian. I enjoy the challenge of the mystery and the excitement of discovery when I search for my ancestors. I still have the first pedigree chart I developed as part of 9th grade English assignment. That was over 40 years ago. I have seen more advances in access to information in the past five years than I saw in the preceding 35 years.

Ten things I hope will happen

As you read this book I hope you get something you can use to help create better service for the genealogists that come to your library.

1. I hope this book will change the way you see the information needs of family history researchers.

2. I hope you will develop a greater appreciation for your role as a librarian who helps genealogists.

3. I hope you will discover some genealogical resources you have never seen before.

4. I hope you will get some good ideas for helping beginning genealogists.

5. I hope you will feel empowered to contact other agencies for genealogical information.

6. I hope you will learn and share with your patrons the genealogical research process.

7. I hope you will learn how the Internet can enhance family history research.

8. I hope you will discover some books you can't wait to order for your library.

9. I hope you will get the facts you need to help your patrons select genealogy software for their computers.

10. I hope you will get so excited about genealogy that you will begin research on your own family tree.

Most of all I hope you will enjoy reading this book as you discover new ideas and new ways to serve genealogists.

Chapter 1

The Hunt through History

*E*very year thousands of people everywhere begin searching for their ancestors. For many, this search will eventually bring them to the library. How librarians see this opportunity will make a tremendous difference to their customers. Through the library door genealogists can have access not only to local information and collections, but also to the vast and sometimes very specialized holdings of resource centers around the world. In this chapter I will give you a quick overview of the information and records people are seeking in order to extend their family trees and some of the many places where they may find them. In chapter 2 the search becomes more structured with the addition of the Genealogical Research Process, a series of research steps that help searchers to work through the confusing process of organizing their research. Recording what you know and where you found it plays a large role in the quality and extent of the genealogical pedigree. Chapter 3 provides the basic forms every genealogist needs for recording and organizing the family information they gather and some of the basic tools for success.

Together, these three chapters lay the groundwork for understanding the tools, resources and services that are described in the rest of this book.

The Information Researchers Are Looking For

When a genealogist walks into a library, he or she will be looking for very specific information. This data will link information he or she has about an ancestor to additional information about that ancestor. Sometimes this information will be a death date, a marriage date, a birth date, or even information about siblings. Each piece of information is like the piece of a puzzle; when all put together they render a complete picture. Genealogy becomes addictive because there is always another piece to the puzzle that still needs to be found.

Identifying and Ranking Genealogical Sources

With the immense historic fabric that must be examined for the few threads that genealogists seek, a ranking of the records based on the quality of the information they contain is essential. When dealing with historic records, most historians and genealogists begin by classifying records as either primary or secondary documents. *Primary records* are those documents that were created at the time of the event by someone who witnessed the event. Even within this category of records there are gradations of quality. Primary records like church and vital records, which provide names, dates, and family relationships, are the type of records every genealogist hopes to find. Other records like immigration/emigration, probate, military records, tax lists, school, and pension records are still primary sources, but they often lack the names, birth and death dates, and relationships needed to add to the family record.

Secondary records are those sources that have been created from primary records or by people who were not there when the event occurred. A will is a primary source. So is a death certificate, but only to the fact of the place and date of death. The other types of the information on a death certificate (birthdate, birthplace, parents, etc.) are secondary records. A county history or a family group sheet are secondary sources because they are more than likely created from more than one source by someone who was not there when all of the events occurred. These distinctions are important when it comes to resolving conflicts between two different records. The primary source will usually take precedence over other sources.

Ranking Records for Reliability

While it is essential to recognize whether we are working with a primary or secondary document, other ways of labeling sources may be more helpful. Consider the following as a ranking of reliability.

1 Original records.
2 Copies of original records (including photocopies and microfilm).
3 Extracted records (including typewritten copies of original records).
4 Compiled records with documentation.
5 Compiled records without documentation.

I must caution that this list should not be considered an absolute rule. A researcher may find an original record, but the document may be unreadable. I have seen writing on deteriorated paper where the ink had faded so much that no one could read it. Some census microfilms are so light they can't be read, and the handwriting on some wills is so bad that it takes special skill and a lot of time to read them. Microfilm copies of original documents may be unreadable because they are too dark, and extracted documents may carry human or typographical errors. With these possible problems in mind, the list above still can be very useful to researchers in comparing the relative value of information they find in various types of records.

Non-Genealogical Sources

Many valuable reference tools were not created with a genealogical purpose in mind. They cannot be expected to offer generations of family records in a page or two, but the information they do provide can serve as clues to more productive sources. Land records are a good example. A father and mother may deed a piece of land to a son or daughter. That deed may be the only record available that proves the parent-child relationship.

In another example, a genealogist had a photograph that had been handed down to him. The photo was of two people—a man and a woman who appeared to be in their early twenties. There were no names on the back, only a faint stamp of the photographic studio on the face of the photograph. On very careful examination the researcher could see a year and the city of the studio. When he searched the county records for the year and the city he found a marriage record for his great-great-grandparents. The photo didn't have an index or any names, but it was a very valuable clue to finding an important piece of genealogical evidence.

Important Genealogical Sources and Where to Find Them

In solving the puzzles of family history, you will find yourself guiding researchers through both the use of sources very near at hand and those that are in remote libraries and archives. The chart that follows on pages 14–15 is designed to identify the most important sources and their possible locations. In order to make this information more useful, there are a few things I would like to say about these sources and agencies.

Personal/Family: While it is not likely that individuals will have many of the types of records listed, it is possible that they will have some of them. It is highly likely that families will have records like a family Bible, birth, death and marriage records, as well as documentation for events that might have influenced a life of an ancestor. Immigration, naturalization, name changes, divorces, baptismal certificates and adoption decrees are very likely to be found among personal possessions.

Local Libraries: The genealogical holdings of local libraries can vary widely. It is reasonable to expect that any place that calls itself a public library should have at least those materials published on local citizens.

Other Local Agencies: Included here are county courthouses, local museums, mortuaries, cemeteries, and historical and genealogical associations.

State Archives: These agencies are sometimes part of the state library and sometimes they are separate. They are generally open to the public and often have newspapers on microfilm and original vital records not housed at county courthouses.

National Libraries/Archives: These facilities have a global perspective. They were established with very specific goals and have significant resources. Although they were not created with genealogist's needs in mind, their large collections are well-indexed and access is usually very good.

Family History Library: This library is in a class all by itself, not because it is the largest library of its kind in the world, but because of its vast network of branch libraries or Family History Centers—one of which may be near to your library. The Family History Library has a tremendous variety of record types.

Visualizing Levels of Collection Development

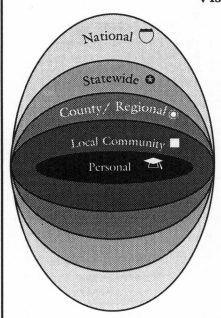

You will find many bibliographic references to genealogical materials in this book. These will include everything from guides and indexes for special collections to general how-to handbooks. Some of the materials are more appropriate for larger libraries with substantial budgets, and others belong in any size collection, even in the personal research collection.

To help you identify materials most appropriate for your collection, I have created this graphic to illustrate the levels of collection development and assigned symbols to each level. Whenever appropriate, the sources listed throughout the rest of the book will be identified with these symbols. They are: 1) Materials appropriate for the average genealogist's personal collection are designated with ☂. 2) Materials for a local library will be designated with ■ . 3) Materials for a county/regional library will be marked with ◉ ; 4) for a state library with state-wide responsibilities ✪; 5) and for a library with national responsibilities ○. It is assumed that resources appropriate for one level will also be appropriate for the levels above it.

Genealogical Source Guide

Genealogical Resource	Personal/ Family	Local Library	Local Agencies	State Archives	National Archives	Family History Lib
Adoption records	X		X	X		X
Ancestral File		X				X
Atlases	X	X	X	X	X	X
Bible records	X			X	X	X
Bibliographies		X	X	X	X	X
Biographical Dictionaries		X		X	X	X
Biographical Directories		X		X	X	X
Biographies	X	X		X	X	X
Catalogs		X		X	X	X
Cemetery Records	X	X	X	X		X
Census Records	X	X	X	X	X	X
Censuses of Manufacturers				X	X	X
Church history		X	X	X	X	X
Church records (baptisms, marriages, deaths)			X	X	X	X
Church records (family books)	X		X	X	X	X
Church records (membership lists)			X	X	X	X
City directories		X		X	X	X
County Courthouse Records				X		X
County histories		X	X	X		X
Court records	X		X	X	X	X
Diaries	X		X	X		X
Directories		X		X	X	X
Emigration/Immigration	X		X	X	X	X
Employment	X			X	X	X
Family Group Records Collection						X
Family histories	X	X	X		X	X
Federal Census		X		X	X	X
Federal Courts					X	X
Fire Insurance Maps			X	X	X	X
Genealogies	X	X	X	X	X	X
Guardianship	X		X	X		X
Guides - Genealogical	X	X			X	X
Guides - Internet	X	X				
Headstone Inscriptions	X	X	X			X
Heraldry	X	X				X
Immigration	X			X	X	X
Index to Institutions 1880-1920					X	X
International Genealogical Index (IGI)		X			X	X
Internet Searches	X	X			X	X
Journals & Diaries	X			X	X	X

Genealogical Source Guide

Genealogical Resource	Personal/ Family	Local Library	Local Agencies	State Archives	National Archives	Family History Lib
Land and Property Records			X	X	X	X
Lineage Books		X	X	X	X	X
Local Government Records			X	X	X	X
Magazines (Electronic)	X	X				
Mailing Lists	X	X				
Manuscript Collections				X	X	X
Maps	X	X	X	X	X	X
Medical records			X	X	X	X
Migration				X	X	X
Military Pension Records	X			X	X	X
Military/Naval Censuses					X	X
Mortality Schedules		X		X	X	X
Mortuary Records			X	X	X	X
Name Changes				X		X
Native Races	X	X	X	X	X	X
Naturalization	X			X	X	X
Newsgroups	X	X			X	
Newspapers	X	X		X	X	X
Obituaries	X	X	X	X	X	X
Oral histories	X	X		X	X	
Passenger Lists		X	X	X	X	X
Periodicals	X	X	X	X	X	X
Photographs	X			X	X	
Postal Records				X	X	
Probate Records	X	X	X	X	X	X
Public Lands			X	X	X	X
Public Records			X	X	X	X
Religious Organization Records				X	X	X
Revolutionary Pensioners		X		X	X	X
School Records	X			X	X	X
Scrapbooks	X	X	X	State	National	
Sexton Records			X	X	X	X
Slave Schedules		X		X	X	X
Social Security Death Records		?			X	X
State Censuses		X	X	X		X
Tax Records			X	X	X	X
Union Veterans and Widows Pension 1890			X	X	X	X
Vital records-Births	X		X	X	X	X
Vital records-Deaths	X		X	X	X	X
Vital records-Marriages	X	X	X	X	X	X
Voting Registers			X	X	X	X
Wills	X		X	X	X	X
Yearbooks	X	X	X	X	X	X

A Closer Look at Significant Sources With the Greatest Research Potential

From the Genealogical Source Guide (pp. 14–15), I have selected some of the more important document sources for closer examination.

Adoption Records: These court records are made at the time of the adoption. Availability of records varies from state to state, but most adoption records before 1930 are open to the public. Since then, stricter right-to-privacy laws have made it more difficult to access these records.

Ancestral File: This CD-ROM tool was created by the Family History Library from records submitted by individuals as a tool for genealogical research. It includes individuals linked together in families from generation to generation. A list of submitters' names and addresses is connected to each pedigree. Users can download data in GEDCOM format for transfer to a home computer. Researchers need to recheck the information they find because errors are inherent in this type of tool. (See also p. 28)

Bible Records: These records have been created by individuals in families to record vital statistics of their family. They are considered a primary source document and they usually include marriages, births, and deaths. Family Bible records firmly document the relationships of individuals in a family. They are written (most of the time) by those who were there when the events being recorded happened. Sometimes several entries are made at once after accumulating over a period of months or years. (Despite their generally high level of accuracy, there are times when the actual marriage date or birth of the first child may be altered to hide an out-of-wedlock birth or an underage marriage.) Copies of family Bibles are available on microfilm or microfiche. Many are available through archives and the Family History Library.

Biographical Dictionaries: These reference works were created to tell about the accomplishments of individuals who usually share a common discipline or field. Entries usually contain birth, marriage, family, and death information and often a long list of achievements which can lead to additional research. Information is usually well researched and accurate, though sometimes incomplete. Only the most famous people are included. If they are in-print these dictionaries are readily available from the publishers. If not, look for a reprint or a microfilm copy.

Biographies: Biographies focus on, or tell the story of a person's life. They usually, but not always, include essential genealogical information on the biographee. Sometimes they include details about family members. Biographies are a secondary source that may have errors, and the genealogical data needs to be verified. Biographies of local people should be kept in a local history collection and not circulated.

Cemetery Records: These records are usually copied by volunteers from grave markers for genealogical purposes. The records are compiled into books and are often published by local historical or genealogical societies. The records include birth and death dates for individuals, though sometimes complete dates (month and day) are not available. They sometimes give the names of other family members and their relationships. Cemetery records are usually reliable for a death date and place. Birth dates may be inaccurate and maiden names for women are rarely given. Printed cemetery books are one of the few locally produced records that can be expected in a local public library. They often go out-of-print soon after they are published. Buy more than one copy when they are available.

Census Records: Population schedules were taken by the federal government starting in 1790 and by some states in various years. The purpose of the federal census was for apportionment of representation in the national congress, and for potential military recruitment, and taxation. The 1850 federal census was the first to record the names of a spouse and the children with living parents. The 1840 federal census is good for identifying Revolutionary War pensioners. Birth dates, marriages, and deceased children are missing from these records.

Federal census records are available for rent from the National Archives,

GEDCOM (GEnealogical COMmunication) is a special computer protocol that was developed by genealogists to facilitate transfer of data between different genealogical software and online databases. Any producer of genealogical software products must meet this standard to ensure record compatibility.

Heritage Quest (AGLL), the Family History Library and several other agencies. They are also available for sale. Many libraries have chosen to buy all available census records for their county or state.

Church Records: Christenings (baptisms), marriages, and funerals are sacraments or ordinances in most Christian faiths. They were created by clergy for the church. In early America, ministers and clergy were required to submit their records to civil authorities. Usually accurate, these primary source documents for births, marriages, and deaths can be used in lieu of vital records gathered by the state or county. They often include information on extended families. Most church records are available at the church where they were created. Sometimes Catholic Dioceses have archives with church records for some years.

Church Records—Family Books: These are pure treasures if you can find them. They have been created by clergy to keep track of families. They list the mother and father and all the children. Genealogists can create a family group sheet, including birth, marriage and death, from a single primary record. They even have information on the extended family, often three generations. The best place to look for church family books is the church where they were created or the Family History Library Catalog.

City Directories: Published city directories may be a good way to locate an ancestor, which can lead to finding the person in the census population schedules. Finding an ancestor in a city directory may lead to a marriage or death record. The earliest directories were done in the late 1700s. They became more common in the early 1900s. Many city directories are now available in microform.

County Histories: Many county histories were created by entrepreneurial publishers around the turn of the century as well as at other times. They often contain good general information about the county and its more prominent citizens. They have good clues for settlement and migration patterns. Some have good genealogical data on the people they include. Even though some county histories were written by scholars who spent years compiling their data, many county histories were created by people who were more interested in making money than producing an accurate, well-written record for posterity. Don't count on finding the names of every person who lived in the county; lots of people couldn't afford the cost of being included.

Court Records: Court records are created as a result of some action in a court of law. Some actions of particular interest to genealogists are adoption, guardianship, probate, divorce or custody. Genealogists are interested in the records of the courts such as docket books, minute books, and case files. Docket books can serve as an index to court records. Researchers can scan the docket for a surname, then find the records they need. For every action pertaining to a case, the case number is found by scanning the pages of the minute book for every occurrence of the case number found in the docket book. The case file (or packet) contains all the papers filed in connection with the case. Court records on microfilm can be found in county, state, and federal archives.

Family Histories: Most family histories were created by a family historian who wanted to share his or her efforts with other family members. They have the potential for lots of good information, containing lineages, families, events, dates and places. However, some portions of the families or family skeletons may be omitted because of a family feud or family secrets.

Family Archives by Family Tree Maker: This is a CD-ROM product marketed by Family Tree Maker that is similar to the *Ancestral File*. People submit their genealogies to the producers of Family Tree Maker and they compile the information and put it on a CD-ROM and sell it to libraries and individuals. Errors are inevitable and the information should to be verified.

Guardianship: These are court records kept at the county level or in a state archive. Families may have original records that pertain specifically to their family members.

Proxy ordinances are religious ordinances performed in LDS temples by the living for and on behalf of someone who is deceased.

In some cases guardianship records may be the only place where the parents of an individual are listed. Check the courthouse where the guardianship hearing was held. You may have to prove a relationship to gain access to these records.

International Genealogical Index (IGI): This CD-ROM- and microfiche-formatted database has been created by the Family History Library from records submitted by individuals to LDS temples for proxy ordinances. They have birth and marriage information for deceased individuals. The microfiche are available for sale to libraries and individuals. The CD-ROMs are available at Family History Centers and some libraries. The *IGI* has about 300 million entries. Submission sheets are available on microfilm.

Internet Searches: Every day people are putting their genealogy on the Internet, hoping that others will see it and contact them to share information. The Internet offers more potential for the sharing of genealogical data than any technology since microfilm. Relatively easy access and speedy communication between individuals are two strong points of genealogy on the net.

Journals and Diaries: These primary source documents are as valuable as the information they contain. Some may go on for volumes and never mention a useable genealogical fact, but the sentimental value may be priceless. Diaries or journals may contain touching descriptions of a marriage or courtship or some particularly difficult times for the individual. They may also be laced with omissions or a perspective favorable to the writer. Copies of journals or diaries may be found in archives or large libraries.

Land and Property Records: Because they record and protect a property interest, land records are among the oldest and most pervasive records available. They establish a basis for property taxes, which was the main basis for government revenue in the early days of our country. The problem with most land records is they don't give very much genealogical information. They do establish that the parties involved were in the county at the time of the transaction, and they often provide references to relationships. They also provide clues for other research. Land records are found in county courthouses and state archives.

Lineage Books: Lineage books are created from the applications of individuals who have sought membership in an organization that required proof of lineage for membership, such as the Daughters of the American Revolution. If the record is accurate, the lineage will go back several generations and will reference documented proof of the lineage. Since lineage books only trace the line of one individual, sibling and collateral lines are not included. These books are secondary sources and some inaccuracies are likely to be discovered. The books are generally available from the producing institution. If there is a local chapter of the organization, local members may be willing to give a set to the library.

Manuscript Collections: Manuscripts are usually found in state historical archives or national archives. They include: Bible records, letters, genealogical notes and charts, personal papers, local government records, state government records, church records, cemetery records, business records, military records, organization records, maps, and plans. These are not easy to access, but they often contain information not available from any other source. Check with the state historical society or the National Archives. Also check: *National Union Catalog of Manuscript Collections.* (Washington: Library of Congress, Annual, –1985. Biennial, 1986/1987–1988-89. Annual, 1990–1993).

Military Pension Records: These records provide proof of military service for the purpose of receiving a military pension. Included in the documentation are: state marriage records, children and their birth dates, siblings, birth and death dates and addresses for the soldier and his wife. The papers have lots of birth dates, places, affidavits, etc. This can be a rich resource.

For more information, check out this Web site: **How to Order Military and Pension Records for Union Civil War Veterans from the National Archives:** http://www.oz.net/~cyndihow/pensions.htm. *(Updated 1/29/98) (Accessed 1/30/98)*

Also check *Tracing Your Civil War Ancestor* by Bertram Hawthorne Groene (New York: Ballentine, 1989. ISBN 0-345-36192-X. ◉).

Military Index: Another component of *FamilySearch* is the *Military Index*. The *Military Index* lists individuals in the United States military service who died or were declared dead in Korea or Vietnam (Southeast Asia) from 1950 to 1975.

Mortality Schedules: These list individuals who died the year before the census was taken. A mortality schedule includes: the individual's name, age, sex, occupation, cause of death, date of death, and place of death by county. If an ancestor died in 1849, 1859, 1869 or 1879, they will likely be listed in a mortality schedule. These primary source documents will be found with the census records. They are available through the National Archives, the National Archives regional centers and at many libraries.

Mortuary Records: These records are created by local funeral homes at the time of service. They can be a good source of information. Most entries give the date and place of death, place of burial, spouse's name, place of birth, an obituary, and an itemized list of the funeral and burial expenses. Many funeral homes will give out the information over the telephone, but they need the exact date, at least the month and year. Some mortuary records are available on microfilm. Local libraries often have locally produced indexes.

The easiest way to find a funeral home is to use one of the telephone directories on the Internet, such as **Switchboard:** http://www.switchboard.com/. *(Accessed 1/28/98)* Select "Funeral Directors" from their list of categories. Then type in the city and state where the person died. You may also want to try **FuneralNet Directory:** http://www.funeralnet.com/search.html. *(Accessed 1/30/98)*

Name Changes: If you know that an ancestor lived and died in a certain area and you still can't find anything; or if you know that he or she changed his or her name, look for name change records in the county courthouse where he or she resided. Courthouses and archives are the best sources of these records.

Naturalization and Citizenship: These records are primary source documents that were created by the federal agency that provided citizenship service. Naturalization records provide: the place and date of birth, date of arrival into the United States, residence at the time of naturalization, and a description of the individual. The name of the ship that brought the individual to the U.S. is sometimes listed. For the years 1781 through 1906, naturalization records are available through the National Archives. Records after 1906 are available through the Immigration and Naturalization Service.

Obituaries: Obituaries announce the death of an individual and are a primary source for death date and place. They usually give birth and death dates and marriage information, along with the names of parents and other family members. The birth information they provide is not always reliable. Marriage information may not be reliable either. Obituaries in newspapers are one good source of information regularly found in public libraries—even small ones. Some state archives have undertaken extensive microfilming projects to copy every newspaper in the state.

Oral Histories: These are the stories that living individuals tell about their past, or about the experiences of other people. They are usually collected by family members or serious oral historians. Armed with a tape recorder and a set of questions, collectors of oral history visit the homes of people they believe have valuable stories to tell about the past.

An oral history was the key to establishing the identity of the father of one of my ancestors whose parents were not married. Oral histories are available at libraries and archives, but many are likely to be kept by families in their home records.

Passenger Lists: These lists are important because they help link our immigrant ancestors to their home countries. Sometimes they give us family information that establishes the age, marital status and place of birth of an ancestor. Published passenger lists will appear in books or periodicals. They are often indexed, and many are found in libraries. Unpublished passenger lists may or may not be indexed, and are available primarily from archives.

Passport Applications: The United States started issuing passports in 1795. At first only a few were issued and the applications didn't contain much information of value to genealogists. Around the mid-1800s passports were required and the applications included more information of value to family researchers.

Since the early 1900s passport applications have included the applicant's full name, birth date, birthplace, current residence and dates of departure and destination. Foreign-born applicants needed documented proof of naturalization. Minor children needed the name of the father, his date and place of birth, and proof of the father's naturalization. Physical descriptions were also provided, and many had pictures attached.

This could be a good source of information if an ancestor traveled abroad. Passport applications indexes through 1925 are available at the Family History Library. They are also available from the U.S. State Department and a copy can be obtained for $14 per applicant. Contact the Passport Office, U.S. State Department, 1425 K St., NW, Washington, DC 20520.

Periodicals: Genealogical periodicals contain genealogies, transcripts, abstracts of local records, probate records, church records, and cemetery records. Many periodicals cover specific sections of the country, such as the *William and Mary Quarterly* for Virginia, and the publications of the Genealogical Society of Pennsylvania. Don't overlook locally produced or family association newsletters. They often include extensive genealogies. The best source of periodical information is the Allen County Public Library in Fort Wayne, Indiana (See Allen Country Library, p. 64–65).

Photographs: Photos are valuable primary source documents, though they rarely contain any family data. However, they often provide clues for further research. Sometimes a photograph can tell us more about the people in them than any other source available. It is unlikely that a small library will collect and preserve photographs, but they are commonly found in museums, archives and private collections.

Postal Records: These records may include a box number and individual records kept by the U.S. Postal Service. Files may also include records with private mail carriers. These records may help to locate families or individuals when other finding tools fail. They are good "between censuses" finding tools.

Probate Records: Probate records are important to genealogists because they are some of the earliest documents available. They were created at the time someone died to settle their estate. As such, probate records help document family relationships and dates of death. A will may list the wife and/or husband and all the children by their given names, as well as some grandchildren's names and the married names of daughters and their husbands' names.

If a person owned property, and most people did, there has to be a probate record, even if there was no will. These court records can be found in county courthouses, in state archives or in the Family History Library. If you search long and hard enough you can almost always find some court record of a person's death.

Scrapbooks: Many libraries and archives maintain scrapbook collections that can be a major resource for genealogists. Subjects include churches, people, families, events, businesses, etc. Many scrapbooks are accessible through the library's catalog. Most scrapbooks are one-of-a-kind items and must be used in the library. Unless you have a space or storage problem, don't turn down the gift of a scrapbook.

Sexton Records: A sexton is the person in charge of a cemetery. His records show every grave in the cemetery, even those that are not marked, and record the name of the person buried there. The sexton records are usually kept at the cemetery, often with a copy in the office of the church or city hall. These records are important for those who want to pinpoint the exact location of someone's grave.

Social Security Death Records Index: This is an index of Social Security death records compiled by the Social Security Administration. This index lists about 50 million Americans who died during the period 1962 – 1990, and whose survivors applied for the Social Security burial benefit. It also includes records for 400,000 rail-

---

A 39-page descendancy chart I compiled on Robert Boggess, one of my ancestors, was published in the *Boggess Newsletter*. It contained information many family members didn't have. After it was published, I received a letter from another Boggess researcher who corrected some information I had used from an inaccurate source, and I was able to amend my data.

Once I called the city offices in Ft. Madison, Iowa, to ask how the get information from their cemetery. They looked up the names I wanted and gave me the information over the telephone in about 30 seconds.

The Soundex Code is an indexing system which translates names into a four digit code consisting of one letter and three numbers. The most familiar application of Soundex is its use by the U.S. Bureau of the Census to create an index for individuals listed in the U.S. Census records after 1880.

The amount of information on a birth certificate varies widely. I have four children. Each of them was born in a different state. The birth certificate for my daughter gives the names of her parents and both sets of grandparents. The certificate of one of my sons only states his name, his birth date, and place of birth.

road retirees. It is not a complete index to every person who died between 1962 and 1990, but it is still a tremendous resource. Researchers can find the individual's name and Soundex code, birth date, death date, Social Security Number (SSN) and state where the number was issued. Usually postal zip codes of the individual's last known residence are included. Some of the records contain the zip code of the address where the death benefit was sent. A copy of any deceased person's original application for a Social Security card can be obtained from the Social Security Administration.

The *Social Security Death Records Index* is available on CD-ROM through both the National Archives and is part of the *FamilySearch* suite available at Family History Centers. It is also available for sale from commercial providers.

Tax Records: Tax records can be used for genealogical purposes in lieu of land or census records. They document that a person lived at a certain place on a specific date. They provide a record of lands assessed for taxation showing names of resident and nonresident owners, a legal description of land, number of acres, value of real estate established by the assessor and the equalized value of the land, and the amounts of the several taxes levied on each parcel. Sometimes these records are the only records available to document an ancestor's existence and place or residence. These records are available in county courthouses and state archives.

Vital Records—Births: The purpose of registering births was to establish citizenship, proof of age, and property interest, if any, for the person who was born. The registration of births didn't happen in every county or state at the same time. About the mid-1800s counties in some states began civil registration of births and by 1920 most states required it. However, some states have birth records that go back much further. Some states have gathered all of the birth records in the state, archived them, and made them available on microfilm. In other states, counties still hold the records that were created for the county, and the state holds the records sent to the state. Check the *Family History Library Catalog* on a county by county basis for availability of birth records.

Vital Records—Deaths: Civil registration of deaths somewhat parallels civil registration of births. The main purpose of registering deaths was to establish the basis for a pension from the government and to settle the property interest in an estate. Death certificates are required to claim the benefit of a life insurance policy, to probate a will, or some other Social Security death benefit. Death certificates, like obituaries, are primary sources for the death date and place of the individual. However, they are not entirely reliable regarding birth, marriage and family information. But they do give us clues to other information. Too often, the information you hope will be on a death certificate, like a parent's name or an exact place of birth, is not there.

Death certificates are readily available from the state or county where the death occurred. There is usually a charge of a few dollars. For those who have ancestors who lived and died in Kentucky, the Kentucky Department of Health and Statistics has compiled an index to deaths and mounted it on the Internet. These files contain an index to deaths which have been registered in Kentucky from January 1, 1911 –December 31, 1992. Information in the file includes the name of the deceased, date of death, age at death, and county of death and residence. The original file was produced by the Kentucky Department of Health Statistics, and it is the official data used to generate, among other things, the annual *Kentucky Vital Statistics Report*.

Vital Records—Marriages: Marriage records are some of the earliest vital records available, primarily because of the property interest connected to a marriage. The law of property interest for spouses varies from state to state, but generally a property interest changes when a marriage occurs. On early marriage records the parents' names did not appear in the record, unless the bride or groom were under the age of majority.

Marriage records are available from city, county and state archives. Many marriage books have been compiled and published. They are also published on CD-ROM and on the Internet.

It is important not to discount a particular type of record just because it doesn't have a name, date, place, or event connected to it. Remember, we are detectives looking for the clues to our ancestry.

Wills: Wills preserve and distribute the assets of the owner upon his or her death. These primary documents establish the birth and death of the testator. They often establish the names and relationship of heirs. They name a living spouse and living children. Sometimes they name spouses of adult female children. They usually do not name deceased children. Many wills have been microfilmed and copies are available in county and state archives and the Family History Library.

Yearbooks: University, high school, and middle school yearbooks are good places to find pictures of students who once attended the school. The library should make every effort to collect and preserve any yearbooks they can obtain. If you have them in your collection, keep them in a locked case.

Where to Look First

Genealogists always want to know where they are most likely to find the information they want. With all of the possibilities available it is not easy to give a standard answer that will take them to the best place first. With that caution, the list that follows provides good starting places for these types of information:

Adoption: Try guardianship (court) records, adoption agencies, compiled genealogies, and census records.

Age of a Person: Look in census records, birth, death or marriage records, and cemetery records, military records.

Birth Date: Look in birth records, church records, Bibles, and family records, obituaries, cemeteries, funeral home records.

Birthplace: The first place to look is birth records, followed by census records, church records, family records, and obituaries.

Birthplace, (Foreign City): Try church records, genealogies, naturalization and citizenship first.

Birthplace, (Foreign Country): Look in census records, emigration and immigration records, naturalization and citizenship records, and church records.

Children: First, try census records, birth records, church records, probate records, wills, Bibles and obituaries.

County of Origin: Look in county histories, compiled genealogies.

Death of a Person: Start with death and cemetery records, obituaries, mortuary records, professional directories (e.g. physicians), wills, and probate records.

Divorce of a Couple: Start with court records, marriage and divorce records, and Bibles.

Ethnicity of an Ancestor: First try journals, tribal enrollment for American Indians, and slave rolls (census) for African-Americans.

Immigration Date: Emigration and immigration records, and naturalization and citizenship records are the first places to try.

Living Relatives: Search compiled genealogies, Internet directories, Internet mailing lists, county heritage books, and surname search engines like **Roots-L Surname List**.

Maiden Name: First try marriage records, census records, compiled genealogies, Bibles, wills, probate records, and newspapers.

Marriage: First try marriage and church records, Bibles, newspapers, photographs, wills, land, and court records.

Name Change: Try court records and compiled genealogies.

Parents: First try census records, birth and church records, probate records, oral histories, and obituaries.

Parents of Illegitimate Children: Look first in court records, family histories, family reunions, birth records, and compiled genealogies.

Photos: Contact all living relatives and check county histories, county and state archives, and family Bibles.

Physical Description: Check military records, military draft registration, court records, and biographies.

Places: Look in gazetteers, maps, military records, atlases, census indexes, state indexes, and postal directories.

Previous Research: Check compiled genealogies like the *Ancestral File* and *Family Archives,* the *International Genealogical Index (IGI),* printed genealogies, periodicals, and the Internet.

Religion: The obvious place to check is church records, followed by family and cemetery records, and biographies. Also try Bibles, and genealogies.

Research Outlines

To request the current *Family History Publication List* fill out the order form and send it to:
Salt Lake Distribution Center
1999 West 1700 South
Salt Lake City, Utah 84104-4233

Individuals may order outlines for their own use by calling 1-800-537-5950. They need to have one of the standard credit cards listed on the order form.

Another way to learn where to go first is to use the *Research Outlines* prepared by the Family History Library. In 52 pages or less, these outlines introduce strategies and describe content, uses and availability of major records for specific topics, states or regions. They have an outline for each state which sells for a dollar or less. The entire set for the United States can be purchased for around $25. Prices and content change without notice, but the outlines are updated regularly.

They also have other outlines for foreign countries and areas around the world. These outlines are the most powerful little tools you can buy for your library. If you don't buy anything else I recommend in this book, get all the outlines they offer. Put the outlines in a loose-leaf notebook. Catalog it and put it on the genealogical reference shelf.

The *Research Outlines* have been compiled into a CD-ROM product called *The Family History SourceGuide*® (See p. 45). The paper copy still has its advantages and is worth the money for libraries and serious researchers. Even the smallest libraries should have a copy of the *Research Outline* for their state.

Evaluating Sources

We have already discussed the difference between primary and secondary sources, compiled sources, extracted records, and original documents. Many genealogists don't differentiate between these sources. If the information they want appears in a document that seems to be authentic, they accept it and move on. They probably ought to be more discriminating about some sources they use and question what they see. These questions and responses may help researchers evaluate various genealogical sources.

Checklist for Evaluating a Genealogical Record

1. Did the person who created the record have personal knowledge of the event being recorded?

   A mother reporting a birth record is probably accurate.

2. How long after the event was it recorded?

   Even though family Bible records are primary documents, the records may have been made months or years after the events took place. The longer the time between the event and the recording of the event the greater the possibility for error.

3. Why was the record made?

   Some records have only incidental value, but they may be the only records we have for that place at that time.

4. Does the book or register have an index?

   Indexes make the work easier, but don't ignore a book just because it doesn't have an index. And don't rely solely on the index. Some census indexes have a fifteen to twenty percent error rate.

5. What is the potential for error?

   Any time human eyes and hands come between the original writing of the document and the document you are reading, errors can occur. Even a microfilm copy or a photocopied page can result in errors.

6. Can you read the document?

   It may be in a foreign language. The handwriting may be illegible. The copy may be blurred, too light, or too dark.

7. Can the information be verified?

   If sources are included, you can check the sources, but don't disqualify a piece of information just because you can't check it. Use it as a clue to find corroborating evidence.

8. What is the possibility that the person who gave the information was lying?

   Many spouses who were older than their husband may not want that information to be known, so they could lie about their age.

Summary

It helps to be aware of all the types of records that can be considered relevant for genealogical purposes. It is important to work with reliable records, but the distinction between primary and secondary records is only important to serious researchers. If we have two conflicting records, the one that was written by someone who was present at the event should take precedence.

Suggested Reading

Askin, Jayne, and Molly Davis. *Search: A Handbook for Adoptees and Birthparents*. 2ed. Phoenix: Oryx Press, 1992. ISBN 0897747178. 🎓

Billingsley, Carolyn E. and Desmond W. Allen. *How to Get the Most Out of Death Certificates*, Bryant, Arkansas: Research Associates, 1991

Bremer, Ronald A. *Compendium of Historical Sources: The How and Where of American Genealogy*. Rev. ed., Bountiful, Utah: AGLL, Inc. 1997. ISBN: 1877677159.

Eichholz, Alice, ed. *Ancestry's Red Book: American State, County & Town Sources*. Salt Lake City, Utah: Ancestry, 1992. ISBN 0-916489-47-7. ◉

Rillera, Mary Jo. *The Adoption Searchbook: Techniques for Tracing People*. 3d rev. ed. Westminster, California: Pure Inc., 1991. ISBN: 0910143005. ◉

Szucs, Loretta and Sandra Leubking, comp. *The Source: A Guidebook of American Genealogy*. Salt Lake City: Utah, Ancestry, 1997. ISBN: 0-916489-67-1. ◉

Thorndale, William, and William Dollarhide. *Map Guide to the U.S. Federal Censuses 1790-1920*. Baltimore, Maryland: Genealogical Publishing, 1995. ISBN: 0806311886. ∎

Chapter 2

The Genealogical Research Process

Conducting genealogical research requires a methodical procedure. Without this careful process, errors will occur. Facts will be missed. Research will have to be repeated. If librarians understand the genealogical research process and encourage their family researchers to follow it, they will be providing a great service. This chapter will be spent discussing that process and the best resources to consult first.

The Genealogical Research Process

1   Collect, organize, and record personal sources.

2   Identify and contact family members for information.

3   Add the information to your charts.

4   Survey compiled sources.

5   Focus on one person in a single area.

6   Identify available resources.

7   Select the most appropriate research tool.

8   Acquire the record.

9   Record the source in the research log.

10   Add the information to the genealogical record form.

11   Evaluate the data and begin the cycle again with no. 5.

---

1 Collect, Organize, and Record Personal Sources

At the start of any genealogical research, searchers should be encouraged to locate information from personal sources. If your new genealogists haven't already done this, consider offering them the checklist on the next page. This long list is sure to give them at least a couple of new ideas about resources they may already have.

2 Identify and Contact Family Members for Information

Be certain other family members are contacted for information. Many researchers are surprised to find that their parents, grandparents, aunts, uncles, or cousins may have already done some genealogical study. Sometimes they have a large box full of information to sort through and organize. For people who have difficulty finding their relatives, here are some key contact sources for finding missing family members.

Checklist of Personal Genealogical Sources

Check at home for these items.

_____ Abstracts of title	_____ Engagement announcements	_____ Military service record
_____ Accident reports	_____ Family Bible	_____ Military uniform
_____ Achievements	_____ Family group sheets	_____ Minister's records
_____ Administrations of wills	_____ Family heirlooms	_____ Mission reports
_____ Adoption papers	_____ Family histories	_____ Mortgages
_____ Anniversary announcements	_____ Family records	_____ Motor vehicle registration
_____ Annulment decrees	_____ Farm records	_____ National guard records
_____ Apprenticeship diplomas	_____ Fire insurance policies	_____ Naturalization logbooks
_____ Auction receipts	_____ Firearm registration	_____ Newspaper clippings
_____ Automobile insurance	_____ Funeral programs	_____ Obituaries
_____ Awards	_____ Funeral home receipts	_____ Ordination certificates
_____ Baby books	_____ Genealogical records	_____ Passenger lists
_____ Bankruptcy filings	_____ Graduation programs	_____ Passports
_____ Baptism certificate	_____ Guardianship documents	_____ Pedigrees charts
_____ Biographies	_____ Health records	_____ Pension applications
_____ Birth announcements	_____ Historical society membership	_____ Personal interviews
_____ Blessing certificates	_____ Honor roll recognition	_____ Personal papers
_____ Bonds	_____ Hospital receipts	_____ Personal property tax records
_____ Burial reports	_____ Hospital records	_____ Personnel records
_____ Business license	_____ Hunting license	_____ Probate inventories
_____ Case files	_____ Immigrant records	_____ Probate records
_____ Cemetery records	_____ Immunization certificates	_____ Professional certificates
_____ Charitable donations	_____ Income tax records	_____ Property leases
_____ Christening certificate	_____ Institutional records	_____ Property settlements
_____ Church membership lists	_____ Insurance papers	_____ Property surveys
_____ Church minutes	_____ Job transfers	_____ Publications
_____ Church records	_____ Journals, diaries	_____ Real estate tax records
_____ Church transfers	_____ Judicial summons	_____ Report cards
_____ Citizenship papers	_____ Land grants	_____ Retirement applications
_____ Club dues	_____ Land patents	_____ Scholarship applications
_____ Club membership records	_____ Legal papers	_____ School tax records
_____ College applications	_____ Letters	_____ School transcripts
_____ Confirmation certificates	_____ Library cards	_____ Scrapbooks
_____ Contracts	_____ Life insurance	_____ Secondary school registration
_____ Correspondence	_____ Loan applications	_____ Selective service cards
_____ Court dockets	_____ Marine insurance	_____ Service awards
_____ Court judgments	_____ Marriage announcements	_____ Sextons records
_____ Court minutes	_____ Marriage applications	_____ Social security card
_____ Court subpoenas	_____ Marriage certificates	_____ Tax notices
_____ Criminal convictions	_____ Marriage licenses	_____ Tombstone rubbings
_____ Customs records	_____ Medical checkups	_____ Traffic tickets
_____ Death certificates	_____ Medical records	_____ Union dues book
_____ Deeds	_____ Military citations	_____ Vaccination records
_____ Diplomas	_____ Military disability papers	_____ Visas
_____ Divorce documents	_____ Military discharge	_____ Water rights
_____ Drivers license	_____ Military firearms	_____ Wedding books
_____ Economic records	_____ Military pension	_____ Wills
_____ Elementary school registration	_____ Military records	_____ X-rays
_____ Employment applications	_____ Military separation papers	_____ Yearbooks
_____ Employment termination	_____ Military service medals	

Key Family Contact Sources

Ask relatives   Check with relatives to determine if they know whether other relatives are doing genealogical research. Some might have family stories to share. These family stories, even if they don't provide a birth date, might give a clue that can lead to a gold mine of information.

Use telephone directories on the Internet   The Internet is available in many libraries. If your library doesn't have it now, it will some day soon. Thousands of people have been able to find long-lost relatives by checking one of these directories:

Switchboard: http://www.switchboard.com *(Accessed1/28/98)*

Yahoo People Search: http://www.yahoo.com/search/people/ *(Accessed 1/28/98)*

InfoSpace: http://www.infospace.com/ *(Accessed 1/28/98)*

SalesLeadsUSA: http://www.lookupusa.com/ *(Accessed 1/28/98)*

Whowhere?: http://www.whowhere.com/Phone *(Accessed 1/28/98)*

Use Internet search engines   A person's name can be entered as a search term on any of the Internet search engines such as Yahoo (http://www.yahoo.com) or Alta Vista (http://www.altavista.digital.com). If the person has a home page or is mentioned in a document that has been mounted and indexed on the Internet, the search engine could help find the person.

About six months after I put my personal home page on the Web, I received an email message from a cousin that I had not heard from in about 40 years. He had been surfing the Internet and had found my page by chance. In a nice long letter he told me what he was doing, and I offered to share my genealogy with him.

Try Roots-L Interactive Surname List   Roots-L is a listserv. Genealogists submit surnames they are actively researching, and usually include their email address. Researchers use the search engine by typing the surname in one space and the two letter code for the state in another space.

For example, if someone typed my surname "Swan" and "NY," they would get the reply below.

Swan   1600   now   MA>CT>Albany Co.,NY>IL >AZ>CA, USA   jswan

The first column is the surname; the second two columns tell others that I have information from 1600 to the present. The next indicates that the Swan family was in Massachusetts; Connecticut; Albany County, New York; Illinois; Arizona; and California. The last piece of information is the submitter's "handle" or short name. If they click on jswan the Internet program takes them to an email form with the submitter's email address already scripted in the "To:" position. This makes it easy to send me an email message. I found a third cousin in Colorado using this tool. He gave me some information I had been seeking for years.

Hints

When contacting someone for genealogical information it is always wise to:

- Send a self addressed stamped envelope (SASE) with each request for information.
- Give the person as much pertinent information as you have about the person you are researching.
- Don't mention your relationship to the person. Unless you are first cousins it will just confuse the issue.

✎ 3 Add the Information to Your Charts

Help patrons to understand that they need to accurately record everything they find, whether it is a birth record or an obituary, as well as the source of that information.

When you hear from relatives, remember to add their information to your pedigree charts (see p. 34) and family group sheets (see p. 36). This step would seem logical, but many beginners forget to record data collected from their relatives. Even if it is just a clue to the next place to look, it needs to be added. This step happens thousands of times and seems to never end. In fact, it is the goal of every genealogist to find another fact to add to the genealogy.

~ 4 Survey Compiled Sources

Genealogical data is generally divided into two categories: **original records** and **compiled records**. Records generated by government agencies such as census, immigration, citizenship, vital records (birth, death and marriage) are original records and are important for verifying the accuracy of your research. Accessing these records is often difficult, especially for beginning researchers. That is why we recommend compiled records in the survey process. Compiled records are abstracted or taken from original sources, as well as family Bibles, genealogies, family histories and legends, and organized into a researcher-friendly format such as a book, magazine article or CD-ROM.

Once a researcher's pedigree chart is as complete as possible, he or she needs to check compiled sources for the people at the end of the pedigree. They usually give specific names, dates, places, and relationships for specific families. These sources take the form of family histories or compiled genealogies. The farther back persons can extend their lines using personal and family sources the greater the chances for finding information from compiled or published sources. The chances of finding a connection in the 1700s is better than finding a connection in the 1800s. Compiled sources are not always accurate, and some of them can only be used as a clue to the next place to look or to verify the information that is given.

Key Compiled Sources

The search process in compiled sources involves two approaches: first, searching by name in compiled genealogies; and second, searching the records of a particular locale by name. The key sources to check are:

FamilySearch™

FamilySearch is a suite of CD-ROM genealogical research products developed by the Family History Department of The Church of Jesus Christ of Latter-day Saints (LDS Church) to expedite family history research. If your library does not have its own access to the *FamilySearch* suite of products, then you need to find the nearest LDS Family History Center and get to know the volunteers who work there. A good start is to ask the Center to give the library staff an orientation to their services. If there isn't a Family History Center in your town, locate the nearest one and include this information on your handout of other places for genealogical research. *(See p.59 for information on Family History Centers and how to locate the nearest Center.)*

The databases in *FamilySearch* include *Ancestral File™*, *International Genealogical Index™*, *Family History Library Catalog™*, *The Social Security Death Index*, and *Military Index*.

Ancestral File The *Ancestral File* is one of the first places to look for compiled genealogies. The following is quoted with permission from the pamphlet, *Using the Ancestral File*:

> *People throughout the world are invited to send their genealogies to Ancestral File, through which the information is made available for research. The file links individuals into pedigrees showing their ancestors and descendants. It contains genealogical information on millions of individuals from many countries. This information includes names, along with dates and places of birth, marriage, and death. Most of the information in the file is about deceased people. The file also contains the names and addresses of individuals who have contributed the information. The file is updated periodically.*

Using the Ancestral File, The Church of Jesus Christ of Latter-day Saints, 3rd ed. 1994. Reprinted with permission. Copyright © 1994 by The Church of Jesus Christ of Latter-day Saints.

International Genealogical Index This index is the largest example of compiled vital records. It lists and gives locations of births and marriages for over 300 million people worldwide.

FamilySearch in Other Libraries

FamilySearch is now available to other libraries. Access has to be open to the public and not used for commercial purposes. Current pricing for the initial setup and annual upgrades and licensing is less than $200. The fee is subject to change. Librarians wishing to have Family Search in their libraries should write a letter to:

Family History Dept.
Family History Center Support Unit
50 East North Temple
Salt Lake City, UT 84150

If you only have $200 in your genealogy budget, spend it on FamilySearch and SearchGuide.

The International Genealogical Index (IGI) *lists several hundred million names of deceased persons from throughout the world. The index does not contain records of living people. Many names in the index come from vital records from the early 1500s to 1885. Others have been submitted by members of The Church of Jesus Christ of Latter-day Saints.*

Individuals listed in the index are not joined in family groups or pedigrees. To see if an individual is listed in a family group or pedigree, check Ancestral File.

You can use the index to find birth, christening, and marriage information.

International Genealogical Index, Family History Library, The Church of Jesus Christ of Latter-day Saints, 1995. Reprinted with permission. Copyright © 1995 by The Church of Jesus Christ of Latter-day Saints.

Family Archive® CDs

Produced and marketed by Family Tree Maker, the *Family Archive CDs* are similar to the *Ancestral File*. The *FamilyFinder Index* indexes all of the *Family Archive CDs*. The information can be downloaded directly to a Family Tree Maker Family File, a GEDCOM file, or copied to the clipboard. *http://www.familytreemaker.com/facds.html (Accessed 1/31/98)*

Internet sources

The Internet is a powerful tool for genealogists. Using it to survey compiled genealogical data is not as easy as going to a single published source, but it has potential for great amounts of information. However, the information is all over the place and you have to learn how to use Internet search engines to find it. Librarians can be especially helpful in assisting genealogists who want to use the Internet. Many libraries now have public access to the Internet.

The easiest way to find an ancestor on the Internet is to go to one of the search engines and type in the surname or full name and add "family" or "genealogy" to the search string. The search may bring up a list longer than you want to sort through. Teach the researcher how to narrow the focus of the search by using (+) or (-) to add or subtract words in the search string.

Some Web sites like Family Tree Maker and Ancestry.com are dedicated to helping genealogists put their data on the Web. Go to these sites and test them so you can help your patrons use these search engines.

❧ 5 Focus on One Person in a Single Area

Surveying genealogies usually involves looking for surnames or individual names. The information the researcher finds may have been compiled by someone who has descended from a different member of the family several generations back. Often details needed by the researcher are not available in the compiled genealogy, but might have been noted in local vital records.

So the next step in the process is to check local vital records of births, deaths, and marriages. But before you can do that you have to narrow the search to one person or family in a specific place during a specific time period. The person you choose is up to you, but I would start where the information is plentiful and easiest to access. Your chances of success will be greater.

The *Family History Library Catalog* and *The Family History SourceGuide*™, both on CD-ROM, are the two best places I know to find what genealogical materials are available and where they can be found.

❧ 6 Identify Available Resources

Sometimes it is a good idea to do a preliminary review of some of the catalogs or resource finding tools to determine if there is sufficient data available to do a fruitful search. For beginning researchers it helps to start where there is the greatest potential for success.

One of my grandfathers came from Harrison County, West Virginia. I was fortunate because the records for that area were plentiful and are available through the Family History Library. I was able to gather great amounts of information on his ancestors and extend my line several generations.

Key Catalogs and Resource Guidebooks

Family History Library Catalog™ If I wanted to find out what records were available for an area of my research, I would go to the *Family History Library Catalog* (on CD-ROM) first. It is probably one of the most valuable genealogical indexes in the world. It is the gateway to the vast resources of the Family History Library. Here are some excerpts from the research outline on the *Catalog.*

> *The* Family History Library Catalog *lists and describes the records, books, microfilms, and microfiche in the Family History Library. It does not contain the actual records, only descriptions of them. The records described in the catalog come from throughout the world, and include census records, birth records, family histories, church registers, and many other record types.*
>
> *The library catalog is available on compact disc and on microfiche, both of which are updated regularly. Check the latest edition of the catalog for the library's newest acquisitions.*
>
> Family History Library Catalog, Family History Library, The Church of Jesus Christ of Latter-day Saints, 1995. Reprinted with permission. Copyright © 1995 by The Church of Jesus Christ of Latter-day Saints.

Heritage Quest Microform Catalog. Bountiful, Utah: Heritage Quest, 1997. 🎓

This valuable resource could be the beginning of a wealth of genealogical material for library patrons. It comprises several volumes, filling three large loose-leaf binders. The *Microform Catalog* is free to members of American Genealogical Lending Library (AGLL, see p.68). Libraries, and other institutions pay a nominal fee. Heritage Quest members and institutions may also rent titles from the extensive collection. The catalog of collections includes: U.S. census records 1790-1920, military records, selected state censuses, surname collections, ship passenger lists, vital records, African American records, special collections, other county records, Canadian censuses, family histories, and Native American records.

Only Heritage Quest members and institutions have rental privileges to the extensive microfilm and fiche collection of over 250,000 titles.

National Archives Microfilm Resources for Research: A Comprehensive Catalog. Washington, DC: National Archives Trust Fund Board, 1987. ISBN 0-911333-34-7. ■

Since 1941, the National Archives has microfilmed federal records of high research interest to make the records available for researchers while preserving the originals from deterioration and damage from handling. Copies of these microfilmed records are sold to the public, making these federal records accessible to libraries, research centers, and individuals.

This catalog is essential for any library that rents or buys microfilm from the National Archives. It lists more than 2,000 microfilm publications. (Distributed by: Scholarly Resources Inc.)

Resource guidebooks

There are also some good books that will list some specific titles for a given area. Here are the ones I like best.

Szucs, Loretta and Sandra Leubking, comp. *The Source: A Guidebook of American Genealogy.* Salt Lake City: Ancestry, 1997. ISBN: 0-916489-67-1. ■

Written by several respected genealogical researchers, this book lists and explains the use of a some of the most significant genealogical research tools available in the United States today. The co-editors have produced a superb and scholarly work. The chapter on "Tracking 20th Century Ancestors" summarizes almost a decade of new resources now available to family researchers. This book will continue to be a "must purchase" source for every genealogist, and libraries should have copies both in circulating and reference collections.

Eichholz, Alice, ed. *Ancestry's Red Book: American State, County and Town Sources.* Salt Lake City: Ancestry, 1992. ISBN 0-916489-47-7. ◉

This book is an extensive guide to useful resources in all of the fifty United States and the District of Columbia. It describes some original, printed, and microfilmed sources. Arranged alphabetically by state, each chapter has the same topical organization. Each chapter begins with a brief discussion of the historical background for the state covered by the chapter. It discusses the records available in each state and how to gain access to them.

7 Select the Most Appropriate Research Tool

If you have a good knowledge of the basic genealogical resources, it will be possible to help the genealogist select the tool that will probably have the information that is needed.

If you are ordering films from the *Family History Library Catalog*, the Heritage Quest *Catalog*, or the National Archives, the description of the film will usually give enough information to tell if the data you want is likely to be on the film. At least you have enough information to order a roll of microfilm. If your great grandfather was born in 1875, in Barton County, Kansas, and you don't know who his parents were, it would be worth obtaining a copy of the 1880 census to see if he is listed with his family. Barton County might also have a birth record that includes the years 1872-1900. The important thing to do is to bracket the years and to look for the best possible source.

Without an index, a roll of microfilm can be an insurmountable obstacle. Several rolls without an index are even worse. Sometimes indexes will be included on the microfilm with the records they index. The library should buy printed indexes, if they are available. Indexes can reduce the search time to a fraction. This is all part of selecting the right document and using available tools to assist with the search.

8 Acquire the Record

If the library doesn't have the record the patron wants, the librarian has an obligation to find where it is and obtain it, or at least help the researcher to get the record. If it is available on interlibrary loan the task is easy—at least most of the time. However, most libraries don't lend their genealogical materials on ILL, so other means may be necessary.

If a library has a book that may have some information a patron wants, and they won't send the book on interlibrary loan, ask them to send a photocopy of the index and the title page. If the index shows a name the patron is seeking, ask the librarian to send a photocopy of the pages referenced in the index.

Another way to get information from another library or research facility is to pay someone in the library to look up the information and send it. Many libraries and archives have policies that establish fees and charges for research and photocopies. In chapters 5 and 6 we provide this information on several libraries and archives. Paying for this type of service has become a way of life for many genealogists. Spending $10 to $25 to get what you need from a library or archive that is 1,500 miles away is a lot cheaper than driving there.

Sometimes buying the book is the easiest way to get the information. Some publishers make a living selling materials to genealogists. The library should collect publishers' catalogs for individuals to use.

In-print books are easy to purchase. Out-of-print books are often difficult to find and acquire. A little known source that I believe has great potential is UMI's Books on Demand service. (*Out-of-Print Books on Demand: Author Guide, 1996.* Ann Arbor, Michigan: University Microfilms International, 1996. ISSN 01936239.) ∎

If you have exhausted every possible source and you still cannot secure a copy of an out-of-print genealogy title, you might suggest that your patron search the extensive collection offered by UMI. The Books on Demand service from UMI offers over

A few years ago I reluctantly bought a county heritage book that was supposed to have something about one of my lines in it. This $60 book had only one paragraph that connected to any of my families. But the good news was the paragraph was written by a cousin I didn't know and he was able to give me more information than I have been able to sort through in two years.

3,800 genealogy and local history titles. UMI has microfilmed these books, and it will produce a photocopy of any title on acid-free paper. This service is not inexpensive, but if you can find a title that is important to someone, that person may be willing to pay a premium just to have the book.

Some titles are also available in a microform format at half the price of the custom printed book. Titles added since 1976 are only available in the printed format.

UMI also has vast holdings of dissertations and newspapers, as well as research collections on genealogy and local history, civil war regimental histories, and many other relevant genealogy topics. Contact UMI for a copy of their catalog. UMI, 300 North Zeeb Rd., P.O. Box 1346, Ann Arbor, MI 48106-1346

9–11 Completing the Cycle

You need to help the genealogist record the source in the research log, add the information in the genealogical record, evaluate the data and begin the cycle again by narrowing the focus of research to one person in a single area at a specific time. The basic forms for completing these tasks are discussed in the next chapter.

Summary

Understanding the genealogical research process is important for librarians who provide reference service to genealogists. Helping your patrons understand it may be the best thing you will ever do for them. While the indexes described in this chapter are invaluable in helping to locate information quickly, bypassing a record because it doesn't have an index may be unwise. These are the challenges that make piecing the genealogical puzzle together a lifelong process.

~ Chapter 3

Recording Family Data

Helping Researchers Get Started

The first thing you do when someone comes to the library and asks for help in finding their great-grandmother is to help them find their great-grandmother. The second thing is to find out where they are in their research and move forward from there.

Sometimes the genealogical researcher will be well organized and walk into the library with a briefcase full of charts. Some will know exactly what they need and what resources to consult. Some may not even need help from the staff. However, many others will come in with nothing except the name of one of their ancestors in their heads or on a scrap of paper.

While some of the advice that follows may not apply to all of the genealogists who come to your library, there are enough genealogists who are just getting started to warrant a few pages here about the basic forms for documenting genealogical research. If they don't have their research organized, you need to help them by providing some basic forms. Whether you charge for the forms or not is your business. You might try giving them the first ones free and charging for additional copies. I have always felt that providing a printout or a blank form is a way of answering a reference question.

This chapter provides the three essential forms for genealogists—the Pedigree Chart, the Family Group Sheet and the Research Log—along with a list of other tools the family researcher may need to acquire. These three forms allow researchers to record the family data they gather and to create a record of sources and questions that have been researched. This includes both successful and unsuccessful searches. The list of sources that did not have a particular piece of information are just as important to record as those that did—saving the researcher the time and effort required to repeat the same unsuccessful search at some point in the future.

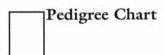**Pedigree Chart**

The pedigree chart is the family tree. You can find one on p. 34. It is the basic form for recording and organizing information about family history. The first pedigree chart a person fills out usually starts with himself, followed by parents, grandparents and great-grandparents, and so on. If more charts are needed the new chart begins with the last person listed on the first chart, giving the potential for eighteen more charts connected to the first.

The name of the husband is customarily recorded in the top half of the bracket. For each individual there is usually a space to record the name, the birth date, the place of birth, the death date, and the place of death. The marriage date and place are recorded under the father. Women's maiden names are always given, if they are known.

Each element of the information about a person provides a clue for additional research. For example, a person's birthplace might be a lead to finding the parents' marriage record. If you can find a marriage record, you might be able to find one or more parents of the couple who were married. Don't assume that these clues always work out. They are just possible leads to be checked out.

The main reason you have your patrons fill out a pedigree chart is to help them organize and record the information they already have. Once this is done you can begin to help them take the next step, looking for clues and sources to check. If they

33

Pedigree Chart

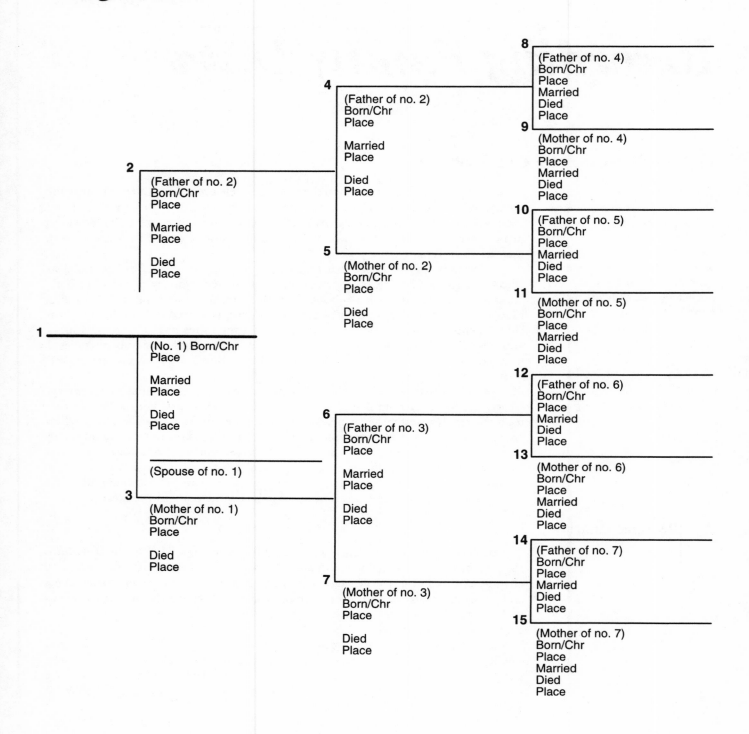

8 (Father of no. 4)
Born/Chr
Place
Married
Died
Place

4 (Father of no. 2)
Born/Chr
Place

Married
Place

Died
Place

9 (Mother of no. 4)
Born/Chr
Place
Married
Died
Place

2 (Father of no. 2)
Born/Chr
Place

Married
Place

Died
Place

5 (Mother of no. 2)
Born/Chr
Place

Died
Place

10 (Father of no. 5)
Born/Chr
Place
Married
Died
Place

11 (Mother of no. 5)
Born/Chr
Place
Married
Died
Place

1

(No. 1) Born/Chr
Place

Married
Place

Died
Place

(Spouse of no. 1)

12 (Father of no. 6)
Born/Chr
Place
Married
Died
Place

6 (Father of no. 3)
Born/Chr
Place

Married
Place

Died
Place

13 (Mother of no. 6)
Born/Chr
Place
Married
Died
Place

3

(Mother of no. 1)
Born/Chr
Place

Died
Place

7 (Mother of no. 3)
Born/Chr
Place

Died
Place

14 (Father of no. 7)
Born/Chr
Place
Married
Died
Place

15 (Mother of no. 7)
Born/Chr
Place
Married
Died
Place

have a death date but no birth information, you can lead them to cemetery records or obituaries from newspapers which may have clues to birth information. You help the patron move methodically from the general to the more specific.

Try linking different types of records together. A patron once came into the library and asked to see the cemetery records. She found the two ancestors she was seeking right away. She recorded the information in her notebook and was ready to leave when I suggested that she look for an obituary in the newspapers we have on microfilm. Within 30 minutes she had found obituaries for both individuals and was able to extend the pedigree of those two people another generation. She was also able to find the names of brothers and sisters of the ancestor.

Family Group Sheet

The next essential form is the family group sheet. While some people are only interested in their direct lineage (that does not include siblings of their ancestors), most genealogists keep track of all people in a family group because the number of children and their names represent proof of family connections. If your genealogical researchers do not have family group sheet forms you can supply one to help them get started. A sample form is on p.36. This form usually provides space to record information on three generations: 1) the husband and wife, 2) the parents of the husband and wife, and 3) the children. The same information requested for each person on the pedigree chart will be requested again on the family group sheet. (This repetition of information is a good reason to use a computer to record and manage genealogical data.) Additionally there will be a space to record the spouses and marriage date for each of the children.

Research Log

Effective documentation requires a research log. Genealogists look at thousands of records, and they don't always find information they can use. Because of this, they need to record every source they check in a research log so they don't repeat their research. This researcher's tool can save time and money. A sample research log is found on p. 37. The bibliographic record can be sources that have been checked for a particular name or date. For example, a person might check a county census record for the Smith family and may or may not find them. The fact that the search was made needs to be recorded. The fact that they didn't find the family may be almost as important as finding it.

Documentation

Librarians who help their patrons do a good job of documenting their sources are doing them a huge favor that will save them time in the future. Documentation is usually recorded on the family group sheet. This information is critical because it helps others who may want to independently verify the information the researcher has recorded. It can also provide the genealogist with a clue for further research. Sources are listed in abbreviated forms. Sometimes a microfilm number and the type of record will suffice. For example, you might see the following: "Fam. Rec. #0165544" sometimes followed by a brief note detailing the actual information cited. Full bibliographic records are not always found on genealogy charts, but should be kept in the research log.

The best book I have ever seen on documenting sources is *Evidence! Citation and Analysis for the Family Historian* by Elizabeth Shown Mills. It sets forth the standard for correct form for source citation and the reliable analysis of evidence. These two practices are inseparable in successful genealogical research. The author's keen observations and approach to this concept is insightful. I would have a copy of this book in circulation as well as in reference.

Some genealogists may have different standards or no standards at all for documenting and proving sources. Others may be seeking membership in a patriotic society and they will have their own high standards of proof and documentation. As a librarian all you can do is have the books that explain documentation and show them to the patrons when they ask.

Family Group Sheet

HUSBAND'S NAME _____

Born (Date) _____ (Place) _____
Married (Date) _____ (Place) _____
Died (Date) _____ (Place) _____   **Your Name & Address**
_____

Father of Husband _____
Born (Date) _____ (Place) _____   _____
Married (Date) _____ (Place) _____
Died (Date) _____ (Place) _____   **Sources, Notes, Etc.**
_____

Mother of Husband _____
Born (Date) _____ (Place) _____   _____
Married (Date) _____ (Place) _____   _____
Died (Date) _____ (Place) _____   _____

WIFE'S NAME _____
_____
Born (Date) _____ (Place) _____   _____
Died (Date) _____ (Place) _____   _____

Father of Wife _____
Born (Date) _____ (Place) _____   _____
Married (Date) _____ (Place) _____   _____
Died (Date) _____ (Place) _____   _____

Mother of Wife _____
Born (Date) _____ (Place) _____
Died (Date) _____ (Place) _____

CHILDREN

	BORN Date Place	DIED Date Place	MARRIED To whom Date
1 M F			
2 M F			
3 M F			
4 M F			
5 M F			
6 M F			
7 M F			
8 M F			
9 M F			

Research Log

Ancestor's Name _____

Objective			Approximate Date	Locality	
Date of Search Number	Location/ Call Numbers	Description of Source (Author, title, year, pages)		Comments/Results (Purpose of search, years, names)	Document names

Additional notes:

Years later the genealogist could be searching again for the same family. Without the research log the person might not remember the previous search and spend hours doing the same work over again.

These three forms are the basis for beginning any family research. The librarian who provides them to patrons is doing a great service. Many other forms are available for a variety of other purposes. The book, *Unpuzzling Your Past Workbook: Essential Forms and Letters for All Genealogists* by Emily Ann Croom (p.46), has many, many forms for genealogists.

Helping Patrons Organize Information

In a very real sense the librarian is a teacher who will be much appreciated for taking time with beginning genealogists to help them get started right.

It will not always be sufficient to give patrons the forms and tell them to go home and fill them out. You may need to coach individuals as they record the information they have collected onto pedigree charts or family group sheets.

Women's names are always recorded with their maiden names if the name is known. If a researcher has found a Mary Smith, who is the wife of John Smith, and it is definitely known that Smith was not her maiden name, no last name should be recorded. If it is known for certain that her maiden name was Smith, her last name should be underlined like this: Mary Smith.

Some genealogical computer software programs automatically write last names entirely in capital letters. This protocol makes it easier to identify last names. Encourage your patrons to follow this format when they write the names of their ancestors on their charts.

Even though there are different styles for recording dates, the standard default format used by many software programs is: day, month (abbreviated to three letters) and year. For example, 11 Jan 1898. This method of recording dates separates the numbers from the letters and avoids the need for a comma between the numbers, as in April 1, 1900. Commas can be mistaken for the numeral 1 or 7. If all dates are written using the same format there will be no confusion.

Places are recorded city first, followed by the county (without the word "county" or the abbreviation "Co."), followed by the state (spelled out). Example: Chicago, Cook, Illinois. Some people have gone to the two letter postal abbreviation for the state, but I prefer spelling out the whole word. Standardization of this format will avoid confusion.

Place of burial does not refer to the cemetery. It refers to the city, county, and state where the individual died. It may be helpful in later research if the cemetery is known to enter it on the family group sheet or in the notes. The cause of death is not usually recorded unless the information might be helpful in tracking genetic conditions for medical reasons. If it is collected, it should be recorded in the notes.

Assessing the Information

Once your patron has all the information recorded on the pedigree chart and family group sheets, it is time to evaluate the data and develop a strategy for future research. Using the Genealogical Research Process discussed in chapter 2, help the patron select an ancestor to pursue. If you know your library's collection well, you will able to suggest places to start. If the patron wants to start in an area where you have no resource documents, there are many other state, regional and national resources for your extended search suggested throughout this book.

Toolbox for Genealogists

Some genealogists may already have most of these tools, but many beginners will not. A librarian can suggest these as it seems appropriate.

Basic List
- printed forms: pedigree charts, family group sheets, research logs, individual checklists, correspondence log, etc.

- loose-leaf notebooks (three-ring binders), one for each grandparent, and more as needed
- softcover loose-leaf books for current research
- a briefcase or tote to carry papers when doing research
- a magnifier for "difficult to read" documents
- postage stamps, and stationery for writing letters
- personal address/telephone directory for genealogy contacts
- personal library of how-to-do-it books and research tools
- a budget for renting microfilm, interlibrary loan costs, etc.

Bigger Stuff

- typewriter or word processor
- personal photocopier
- camera
- filing cabinet
- personal computer workstation with printer, scanner, and genealogical software
- connection to the Internet with email capabilities
- personal microfilm machine

The library should have some items such as a photocopy machine, microfilm reader, and a computer. The patron may be able to avoid the need to buy them.

Most of all, people who are just getting started in genealogical research need to realize that they will have to spend some money to get the tools and resources they need. Tools are not the end in themselves, but the means to an end. Good tools can help us accomplish our goals with less effort and time.

Summary

We have to take our time when we help genealogists who are just getting started, but if we do a good job we may witness great joy and excitement. Having the necessary forms is a great first step. Suggesting places to start looking may be the best thing we can do. Doing a good job on the reference interview will help your patron learn how to ask questions.

Now that we have explored the many types of documents available for genealogical research, reviewed the research process, and helped the patrons get started, we can move to the next level which is developing the collection in the local library and learning how to access the collections of other facilities.

We start by looking at our own mission statement to see where genealogy fits in the total picture. It also helps to understand the missions of other research facilities, because not all of them focus on the needs of genealogists. If we understand how they do business, we can shape our efforts to more closely match what they do best. We win. They win. And our customers win.

Suggested Reading

Croom, Emily Anne. *Unpuzzling Your Past Workbook: Essential Forms and Letters for All Genealogists.* Cincinnati, Ohio: Betterway Books, 1996. ISBN: 155870423X.

Mills, Elizabeth Shown. *Evidence! Citation and Analysis for the Family Historian.* Baltimore: Genealogical Publishing, 1997. ISBN 0-8063-1543-1.

Chapter 4

Developing Your Genealogical Collection

*E*very public library has an absolute responsibility to collect and preserve local histories, newspapers, city directories, telephone directories, etc. Beyond that, those who govern and administer the library have the authority to define the library's policies on the development of its genealogical collection. It may not be possible to set aside a fixed amount in the budget for local history and genealogical materials, but local materials should have a high enough priority so that they don't have to compete with bestsellers for funds. Local materials go out-of-print so fast that the librarian who hesitates may miss the opportunity buy them.

Genealogical Toolbox for Librarians

A plumber would never go to a job without a toolbox. Librarians who help genealogists need toolboxes, too. Most of us think of books and microfilm as the tools of the trade. They are, but there are others that are just as crucial to our efforts. Here are a few to ponder:

Important but less tangible items

The first collection development decision a librarian needs to make is what role the library will have in collecting and preserving local history and genealogical materials.

- **A vision statement for the library that defines the scope of the library's genealogical service.** This can be a sentence within the library's overall mission statement.

- **A materials selection policy that specifically addresses genealogical and local history needs.** This is usually a sentence in the library's collection development policy that says what the library's plans are for developing the local history and genealogical collection. It may include a statement that will guide the librarian and board at budget time.

- **A budget priority that assures that an appropriate share of the library's resources will be allocated and spent on genealogical and local history materials.** Some library budgets have a specific line item for materials in the local history and genealogy section of the library.

- **An interlibrary loan policy that is friendly to genealogists.** Many libraries will lend, through interlibrary loan, county histories or genealogies if they have a second copy. Other libraries will lend microfilm if it can be replaced.

- **A staff that is trained to help genealogists.** Some of the best-trained reference librarians around lack the skills to help genealogists. Even though they can usually do an adequate job, it is best if they can receive some special training on helping with genealogical research.

- **Public relations support to promote the library's service to genealogists.** Too often the library's service to genealogists is almost hidden. That may be because the service is not part of the mainstream service. The Allen County Public Library in Fort Wayne, Indiana, knows how to use its service to genealogists to promote the whole library.

More tangible tools

- **Forms and "Getting Started" handouts for beginning genealogists.** For new genealogists the challenges are great. If you can give them a form to fill out or a checklist to complete, they will feel their trip to the library was successful in helping them to get to the next step in their research. Give them something they can use and they will keep coming back.

- **A detailed brochure that outlines the library's resources for genealogical researchers.** The library's catalog is usually the window to the collection, but if a genealogist doesn't know a tool exists, he or she may miss it in the catalog. Include as many of the types of resources in your library as will fit in the brochure.

- **A way to control the lighting in the microfilm reading area.** Microfilms are sometimes difficult to read if the ambient light is too bright to allow for good contrast on the reading surface of the microfilm reader. Try to figure out a way to reduce the lighting in the area where microfilms are being read.

The big stuff

- **At least one microfilm/microfiche reader/printer.** If the library has a significant microform collection and doesn't have a reader/printer, you are seriously limiting the use of the collection. While these machines may cost a few thousand dollars, they are usually a good target for local fundraising.

- **A photocopy machine in the genealogy room.** If the library can afford a second photocopier, putting it in the genealogy room will be a much appreciated convenience for your genealogists.

- **A computer that is connected to the Internet, and another computer that has a selection of CD-ROMs for genealogical research, and has samples of genealogical software.** Of all the things you could do for genealogist, this could be the most helpful. Genealogy on the Internet is exploding. Researchers are putting their information on the Internet and sharing it with others. If you can afford it, do this one thing and let people know you have a computer for genealogists. They will flock to the library to use it.

Developing the Local Collection

On one of the rare Saturdays I was working reference in the library, three people came in from a town about 60 miles away. They had come to sell the our library a copy of their town history. It was nicely done in the style of a high school yearbook. They apologized for charging $25, but explained that it had cost them $23.75 to produce. I bought the book, and was glad that I did because our service area extends into seventeen counties. I would never have the opportunity to buy it again.

The people who come to your library for genealogical research are more likely to be interested in local materials than they will be in materials from and about other places. It is only after we trace our ancestors back more than a few generations, that the resources we need will be on the eastern states and Europe. Librarians would do well to spend most of their genealogy materials budget on local materials. Many of these materials are found in the list of Significant Sources with the Greatest Research Potential (chapter one, p.16). These locally produced materials may be your best bet. Even though they may have a weak binding or may not have an index, they still contain unique information not available anywhere else. Locally produced cemetery books, marriage records, or obituaries can be the mainstay of your collection because they will have specific names and dates local genealogists need.

Local Resources Every Library Should Have

- city directories and telephone books for as far back as you can collect
- local high school and college yearbooks from day one
- microfilm copies of all available federal and state census records for your county
- cemetery books for the county
- a county plat atlas
- microfilm copies of all newspapers published in your county
- microfilmed courthouse records, if available
- all available local histories for your city and county
- centennial and bi-centennial books for your town and county
- subscriptions to newsletters of local genealogical societies
- county marriage books
- local church histories
- scrapbooks and yearbooks from local organizations
- locally produced oral histories
- collected biographies on local people
- published material from family or military reunions
- a county township atlas
- a state atlas and gazetteer and topographical maps of the state
- a road atlas for the United States
- family histories, especially of families that have lived in the county
- county heritage books
- all available census indexes for your state regardless of format

Locally published materials
A fine example of a very good self-published work is *Baugus, Boggus, & Boggess Footprints on the Sands of Time*, a two-volume set by Joanna Fox and JoAnn Smith. It is the most comprehensive work on this family available. But you cannot order it through Amazon.com. This self-published work is only available from the authors.

For the above list of local materials, simply finding out what is available may be your biggest challenge. Many great genealogy books are not produced by mainstream publishers. Many authors and compilers end up publishing and marketing their own books, and for the librarian, finding self-published books is more difficult. Authors or self-publishers tend to lack marketing skills and the money to advertise nationally. You may be lucky enough to be personally acquainted with the people who are producing local histories. If you serve a wider area, you may not learn about a new book as quickly.

Other Local Agencies and Resources

The first level of resources outside your library is the community. These resources include the courthouse, cemeteries, mortuaries, historical societies, newspapers, etc. You may be able to influence patron access to the information in these agencies by your involvement with the people who run them. If you have regular contact with them, your patrons may have an easier time getting information from them. You will know what they will find if you go to the courthouse yourself and ask the same kinds of questions they will ask.

Helping researchers find the genealogical resources of other community institutions is just as critical to good service as having resources in the library. When I think of resources outside the Great Bend Public Library, the first places I think of are the courthouse and the local Family History Center. I also think of Karen Neuforth, a local genealogist whose language skills baffle all of us. You can probably come up with a list for your own community, and you should.

Information Kit for Patrons
You might prepare an information kit for your patrons that includes a summary of the research process (p. 25), as well as a pedigree chart (p. 34), a family group sheet (p. 36), a research log (p. 37), a checklist of personal genealogical sources (p. 26), and a list of community agencies that have information for genealogists.

Try writing a one-page handout about other places that may have genealogical information. Include the organization's name, contact person's name, the address, telephone number, the hours of service, and a brief description of what they can expect to find or how to use the service. You can pave the way for them by establishing a relationship with the staff in some of these places. Find out what type of information they have and are willing to share. Tell them that you may be sending some genealogists to them from time to time. Only refer patrons who have questions you think the people in these other agencies can answer.

Here are a few places you might want to include on your list:
- **courthouse**
- **LDS Family History Center**
- **funeral homes**
- **newspaper offices**
- **historical societies**
- **churches (especially old ones)**
- **archives**
- **Internet provider (If they want to get online at home)**
- **bookstores**
- **local professional genealogists**
- **local historians**

You may not have the county courthouse in your town. Mention it anyway, it's probably only a few miles away. You may want to include selected businesses, especially mortuaries, in other nearby communities. You may be fortunate enough to have an agency like the State Historical Society nearby. Put them on the list.

Beyond Local Materials

Once you get past local resources you need to think about what other kinds of materials will help your patrons. The level after local resources is the state. If your library is large enough you may be able to collect some of the research tools that cover the state. These resources might include all of the federal census films for your state from 1790 to 1920; or the microfilms of major newspapers in your state. The next level is national. Collection development for this level is beyond the scope of this book.

So many guidebooks like this one assume that the library is starting from scratch in developing a genealogical collection. That is probably not true. Your library may already have many of the titles listed in this book. You can check them off and feel good that you already own them. It will help you to identify where you want to add more resource materials.

The books reviewed here are among the most helpful I could find. The list is by no means exhaustive or complete. It is more of a "first link" list hat will lead readers to the next level of genealogical tools. I have tried to organize the sources into logical groups, but even that doesn't always work. Materials appropriate for the average genealogist's personal collection are designated with [☜]. Materials for a local library will be designated with [■]. Materials for a county/regional library will be marked with [◉]; for a state library with state-wide responsibilities [◎]; and for a library with national responsibilities [○].

Best of the Best

★ *The Handy Book for Genealogists: United States of America*. 8th ed. Logan, Utah: Everton Publishers, 1998. ISBN 1-890895-03-2. (800/443-6325) ☜

This is the best and most sought after guidebook available to genealogical researchers. It belongs in every library as a primary tool for anyone who does genealogical research. Many individuals have their own copy because they use it so much. Librarians may want to have additional copies in their circulating collection.

The Handy Book includes a current, comprehensive list of archives, genealogical libraries, and societies for each state. The lists of valuable printed sources have also been reviewed and updated for this edition. Information for each state follows the same format, with general information on the state, its history, its records, its genealogical societies, libraries, and valuable publications on genealogy in the state.

★ Greenwood, Val D. *The Researcher's Guide to American Genealogy*. 2d ed. Baltimore: Genealogical Publishing, 1990. ISBN: 0-8063-1267-X. ☜

This is the best how-to book for genealogists, though it may cause beginners to stretch a little. It is used as a textbook in college classes, and also serves as a general reference work. This book will teach individuals about genealogical sources—what they contain, how to find them, and how to use them.

This completely revised and enlarged edition is a carefully constructed work on the principles and facts for successful genealogical research, yet it is also a guidebook and field manual, a comprehensive reference book and a textbook. No research is complete without it.

★ *Family History SourceGuide*, (CD-ROM) Salt Lake City: The Church of Jesus Christ of Latter-Day Saints, 1998. Available from: Salt Lake Distribution Center, 1999 West 1700 South, Salt Lake City, Utah 84104. (# 50176)

If you have only $20 to spend on genealogical resources this year, buy this CD-ROM and put it on one of your public access computers. It is the single most powerful genealogical finding tool available at any price. Not only does it reference the resources of the Family History Library, but it also names specific local resources available in each of the states and tells how to access them.

This is an electronic collection of more than 150 research outlines from the Family History Library, and is designed for those who have basic information about their ancestors and now need to be guided to original sources. The hypertext links make it work like an Internet site, enabling users to narrow the focus of their search by clicking on the marked text.

Additional features include: A letter-writing guide to help those writing inquiries in foreign languages, and blank forms and census worksheets that can be printed on a local printer.

How-to Books

Allen, Desmond Walls, and Carolyn Earle Billingsley. *Beginner's Guide to Family History Research*. 3rd ed. Conway, Arkansas: Research Associates, 1997. ISBN: 1-56546-101-0. ☜

The third edition of the *Beginner's Guide* has some important enhancements to bibliography and resource lists, plus significant information about computers and the Internet. It teaches the new researcher the best way to do research right from the start. This book belongs in the circulating collection of every library.

Beller, Susan Provost. *Roots for Kids: A Genealogy Guide for Young People*. Baltimore: Genealogical Publishing, 1997. (Reprint. Originally published: Whitehall, Virginia: Betterway Books) ISBN: 0-80631-525-3. ☜

This how-to-do-it guide is ideal for children. It is an introduction to genealogy with instructions on how to use sources at home and do research at local, state, and national levels. It teaches how to do the research necessary to create a simple family tree. Good for the children's section of the library.

Carlberg, Nancy Ellen. *Climbing the Family Tree with Nancy*. Anaheim, California: Carlberg Press (1782 Beacon Ave., 92804-4515), 1997. ISBN: 0-944878-00-8. 🎓

This is one of the very best books for beginners. Experienced researchers can also benefit from the many suggestions for what to do next. It is a very helpful introductory guide for those who want to get started with their family research.

———. *How to Survive the Genealogy Bug Without Going Broke*. Anaheim, California: Carlberg Press, 1991. ISBN: 0-944878-22-9. 🎓

This little book is packed with many cost-saving tips used by professionals. The money-saving aids include forms for you to copy as needed.

Crandall, Ralph J. *Shaking Your Family Tree: A Basic Guide to Tracing Your Family's Genealogy*. Camden, Maine: Yankee Books, 1988. ISBN: 0-89909-148-2. 🎓

This book targets the needs of amateurs, but many professionals have found it helpful. Clearly written, the material covers nearly every question a genealogist could ask.

Croom, Emily Anne. *The Genealogist's Companion & Sourcebook*. Cincinnati: Betterway Books, 1994. ISBN 1-55870-331-4. 🎓

Many records are waiting to be found, if we only knew where to look. The record keepers of the past—the county clerk, the minister, the ship captain, the census enumerator, the newspaper editor, and perhaps even the friend or neighbor—may have recorded exactly what we want to know. Here, Croom provides helpful signposts for genealogists looking through the records. The author says this is "A beyond-the-basics, hands-on guide to unpuzzling your past." In great detail, *The Genealogist's Companion* examines primary source documents. Part of this book concentrates on special places for research, such as courthouses and public, university, and law libraries, as well as on the genealogical sources available there and how to use them.

The focus is on American research materials created by government and other public agencies, including maps, newspapers, census records, military records, passenger lists, and church records. Readers who want to review foundation sources and basic research methods are encouraged to refer to guides such as *Unpuzzling Your Past*.

———. *Unpuzzling Your Past: A Basic Guide to Genealogy*. 3rd ed. Cincinnati: Betterway Books, 1995. ISBN: 1-55870-396-9. 🎓

This is a great book for beginners. Easy to read and understand, it makes getting started with genealogical research interesting and fun. It's an exceptional guide that is beautifully printed. Make sure the library has copies in reference and in the circulating collection.

———. *Unpuzzling Your Past Workbook: Essential Forms and Letters for All Genealogists*. Cincinnati: Betterway Books, 1996. ISBN: 1-55870-423-X. 🎓

This is a good book for beginners. It has the reproducible forms they need and checklists to help organize their research as well as suggestions to help with the transcription of data from public deed, the marriage record indexes and the census Soundex. The forms for gathering information help save time and create a focus for interviews and research in books, documents, deeds and census records.

The tips on letter writing will make letters more effective. Sample letters provide ideas for letters to individuals, requests for copies of documents, and letters to relatives asking for answers to family history questions.

Dollarhide, William. *Genealogy Starter Kit*. Baltimore: Genealogical Publishing, 1994. ISBN: 0-8063-1410-9. 🎓

Page for page, this little booklet has more help for beginning genealogists than any 32 pages ever written. It gives the names and addresses of specific places to get additional information, including a list of vital records offices for all 50 states and a list of the major genealogical libraries and societies in the United States. Also included are basic master forms.

Flores, Norma P., and Patsy Ludwig. *A Beginner's Guide to Hispanic Genealogy (Introducción a la Investigación Genealógical Latino Americana)*. San Mateo, California: Western Book/Journal Press, 1993. ISBN: 0-936029-31-5. ☜

This guide was especially prepared for beginning genealogists who are researching their Hispanic roots. Text is in both Spanish and English, and includes maps to help with geographical history.

Helmbold, F. Wilbur. *Tracing Your Ancestry: A Step-by-Step Guide to Researching Your Family History*. Birmingham, Alabama: Oxmoor House, 1985. ISBN: 0-8487-0486-X. ☜

Helmbold presents a complete set of directions on how to solve the puzzle of ancestor searching. He deals with planning searches and using common genealogical records. This is a companion volume to *Tracing Your Ancestry Logbook*.

Stryker-Rodda, Harriet. *How to Climb Your Family Tree: Genealogy for Beginners*. Baltimore: Genealogical Publishing, 1993. ISBN 0-8161-5021-4. ☜

Another book targeted at the beginner, *How to Climb* describes how to get started, how to find clues in family mementos, and where to find information about census, church, birth, marriage, death, probate, and land records.

————. *Understanding Colonial Handwriting*. Baltimore: Genealogical Publishing, 1996. ISBN: 0-80631-525-3. ■

Reading original records once we find them is a big hurdle for many researchers. Few people know this better than Harriet Stryker-Rodda, who has developed a simple technique for reading colonial handwriting, which she outlines here. This little book could make the difference between an accurate interpretation and a missed opportunity when working with a difficult original document.

U.S. National Center for Health Statistics. *Where to Write for Vital Records: Births, Deaths, Marriages, and Divorces*. DHHS Pub. No. (PHS) 93-1142. Hyattsville, MD: National Center for Health Statistics, 1993. ISBN 0-160362-75-X. ☜ Available from the Superintendent of Documents, U.S. Government Printing Office, Washington, D.C. 20402. Stock No. 017-022-01196-4.

Whitaker, Beverly DeLong. *Beyond Pedigrees: Organizing and Enhancing Your Work*. Salt Lake City: Ancestry, 1993. ISBN: 0-916489-52-3.

This powerful little book contains hundreds of ingenious tips on how to organize genealogical research. *Beyond Pedigrees* has eighteen full-size, professionally designed charts that can be reproduced. ☜

Guidebooks

Bremer, Ronald A. *Compendium of Historical Sources: The How and Where of American Genealogy*. Rev. ed. Bountiful, Utah: AGLL, 1997. ISBN: 1-877677-15-9.

The book is a unique compilation of genealogical materials. The author has conducted more than a thousand workshops and seminars and has listened to thousands of people raise questions about genealogy. Drawing on these experiences, he has written *Compendium*. This edition has been completely updated with addresses and phone numbers for thousands of genealogical resource centers in America.

Davenport, Robert R. *Hereditary Society Blue Book*. Baltimore: Genealogical Publishing, 1994. ISBN: 0-8063-1398-6. ◉

This publication lists current information on 147 lineage organizations, their officers, and other members. For each listed organization the author gives the name of the society, date of founding, requirements for membership, a mailing address, and the telephone number, where available. This is a valuable tool because the members of these hereditary societies are more than casual genealogists.

DeBartolo, Sharon. *A Genealogist's Guide to Discovering Your Female Ancestors: Special Strategies for Uncovering Hard-to-Find Information about Your Female Lineage.* Cincinnati, Ohio: Betterway Books, 1998. ISBN 1-55870-472-8.

This book will help readers uncover historical facts, personal accounts and recorded events of the women in their ancestries. It is the first guide to offer special strategies for tracing female genealogy. It gives effective methods for determining maiden names and parental lineage. It describes how and where to access official documents that can pinpoint facts about women. It also suggests ways to use personal writings to gain additional insight into female ancestors. The author is a certified genealogical records specialist and has written two other books on genealogy.

Grundset, Eric G., and Steven B. Rhodes. *American Genealogical Research at the DAR.* Washington DC: National Society, Daughters of the American Revolution, 1997. ISBN 0-9602528-9-4. ■

This includes everything you ever wanted to know about the holdings of the DAR. This is a must read for any researcher who plans to go to the DAR Library for research.

Hone, E. Wade. *Land and Property Research in the United States.* Salt Lake City: Ancestry, 1997. ISBN: 0-916489-68-X. ■

Land records are some of the oldest and best-preserved written records in the U.S., and they apply to more people in America than any other written record. Unfortunately, they can also be difficult to understand and use. Researchers often overlook the importance of land records as a source for genealogical information, but significant and often hidden clues can be found in them.

Schaefer, Christina K. *The Center: A Guide to Genealogical Research in the National Capital Area.* Baltimore: Genealogical Publishing, 1996. ISBN: 0-8063-1515-6. ◉

This highlights resources in the Washington, D.C. area, which has some of the most useful and accessible genealogical materials in the country. It discusses the Library of Congress, the National Archives, the National Genealogical Society, the Daughters of the American Revolution (DAR) Library, and many more. It describes each facility and their holdings, and explains how to use them. There is also a list of published indexes and finding aids, key addresses for mail requests, publications, telephone numbers and hours of business, and an itemization of those materials available through the Family History Library system.

————. *Guide to Naturalization Records of The United States.* Baltimore: Genealogical Publishing, 1997. ISBN: 0-8063-1532-6. ◉

Naturalization records are powerful tools to help us find an ancestor who may have immigrated from another country in the last two centuries. This book explains how to use these records. Since any court of record can process naturalization papers, records relating to naturalization can be found in a bewildering variety of courts. This book cuts through the confusion and makes it possible to find naturalization records no matter where they are.

Szucs, Loretto Dennis, and Sandra Hargreaves. *The Archives: A Guide to The National Archives Field Branches.* Salt Lake City: Ancestry, 1988. ISBN: 0-916489-23-X. ◉

This book explains the functions of the Archives and the field branches in seventeen states. The National Archives generally does not have vital statistics, but mainly holds records created by federal agencies.

Tepper, Michael. *American Passenger Arrival Records. A Guide to the Records of Immigrants Arriving at American Ports by Sail and Steam.* Baltimore: Genealogical Publishing, 1996. ISBN: 0-8063-1380-3. ◉

Early immigrants to America often left few traces of their country of origin. However, the information on later immigrants was documented so minutely that the resulting records are among the largest, the most continuous, and most uniform in the nation's archives. Passenger arrival records on the great Atlantic immigration have survived, and they identify the vast majority of persons by name, place of origin, and other particulars. This work looks at the records in their historical and legal framework, and it explains what they contain, where they can be found, and how they can be used.

Thorndale, William, and William Dollarhide. *Map Guide to the U.S. Federal Censuses 1790-1920*. Baltimore: Genealogical Publishing, 1995. ISBN: 0-8063-1188-6. ■

This shows U.S. county boundary maps for the census decades superimposed on modern county boundaries. It gives background information on each census, including census availability for each county.

Directories

Bentley, Elizabeth Petty. *County Courthouse Book*. Baltimore: Genealogical Publishing, 1990. ISBN: 0-8063-1284-X. ◉

In most counties the courthouse is the main repository of court and vital records. This is a reliable guide to courthouses in America. While many county records have been microfilmed and are available at the Family History Library in Salt Lake City, researchers still need current addresses and phone numbers of courthouses across the country. They need information about the coverage and availability of key records such as probate, land and vital records, names of officials, and facts about the range of services available at the courthouse and the cost of such assistance.

———. *Directory of Family Associations*. 3rd ed. Baltimore: Genealogical Publishing, 1996. ISBN: 0-8063-1523-7. ◉

This contains information on approximately 6,500 family name associations in the United States. It lists addresses, telephone numbers, contact persons, and publications (if any). A good tool for the genealogical reference collection. There are many uses for a directory of family associations, but the most obvious is for making contact with family members, sharing information about family history, and discovering who's out there and where you connect on the family tree.

———. *The Genealogist's Address Book*. 3rd ed. Baltimore: Genealogical Publishing, 1995. ISBN 0-8063-1455-9. ■

The information in each edition of *The Genealogist's Address Book* comes from data received in response to direct-mail questionnaires, supplemented by information from printed sources.

The Genealogist's Address Book is a national yellow pages for the genealogist. Classified by subject, cross-referenced and alphabetized, it is a "first link" directory of thousands of key sources of genealogical information. It gives names, addresses, phone numbers, contact persons, and business hours of libraries, archives, genealogical societies, historical societies, government agencies, vital records offices, professional bodies, religious organizations and archives, surname registries, research centers, special interest groups, periodicals, newspaper columns, publishers, booksellers, services, databases, and bulletin boards. This book belongs in every library that serves genealogists.

Directory of Deceased American Physicians 1804-1929. 2 vols. Arthur W. Hafner, Ph.D., ed. Chicago: American Medical Association, 1993. ISBN: 0-89970-527-8. ◉

If your ancestor was a doctor or claimed to be a doctor, this two-volume set may provide information not available anywhere else. It is a guide to over 149,000 medical practitioners, providing brief biographical sketches, including birth and death dates, drawn from the American Medical Association's Deceased Physician Masterfile. It includes indexes to African American practitioners, and self-designated eclectic, homeopathic, and osteopathic practitioners.

Directory of Historical Organizations in the United States and Canada. 14th ed. Mary Bray Wheeler, ed. Nashville: American Association for State and Local History, 1990. ISBN: 0-942063-05-8. ◉

This directory has approximately 13,000 listings. Each part of the directory begins with its own contents page. The product and service section has a self-contained index, alphabetical listing, yellow pages, and a convenient Vendor Fax Finder chart for easy reference. Contents include: Historical Organizations in the United States, Quick Reference Guide to State History Offices, Historical Organizations in Canada, Product and Service Vendors in the United States and Canada, and Quick Reference Index to Major Program Areas. The directory is easy to use and deserves a spot on the reference shelf of all but the smallest of libraries.

Johnson, Richard S. *How to Locate Anyone Who Is or Has Been in the Military, Armed Forces Locator Directory.* Ft. Sam Houston, TX: Military Information Enterprises (P.O. Box 340081, 78234), 1990. ISBN 1-877639-01-X. ◉

This is the only book available with detailed information for finding someone in the military. It reflects many years of research and experience that will save time and expense. It tells the reader:

- how to obtain the unit of assignment, home address, and telephone number of any member of the Army, Navy, Marine Corps, Air Force, Coast Guard, the Reserve Components and National Guard;
- how to locate people through their driver's license or vehicle registration;
- how to have a letter forwarded to a current, former, or retired member of the Armed Forces, Reserves, or National Guard;
- how to have a letter forwarded to any of 27 million veterans;
- how to locate people through the Social Security Administration, the Internal Revenue Service, U.S. Post Office, and other state and federal agencies;
- how to locate former service men and women through veterans' and military associations; and
- how to find out someone's address and telephone number.

Kot, Elizabeth G., and James D. Kot. *United States Cemetery Address Book.* Vallejo, California: Indices Publishing, 1995. ISBN: 0-9641213-2-8. ◉

This work lists 25,000 cemetery addresses and locations, more than any other single source. It also includes any earlier name the cemetery may have had.

Reamy, Martha, and William Reamy, comp. *Index to the Roll of Honor (Civil War).* Baltimore: Genealogical Publishing, 1995. ISBN: 0-8063-1483-4. ▽

This is the index to the most comprehensive source of information on Civil War fatalities. The 27-volumes of *The Roll of Honor* lists burials in over 300 national cemeteries. Searching for individual records in this set was a daunting task until this index was published. A must for any library that has the set: *Roll of Honor. Names of Soldiers Who Died in Defense of the American Union, Interred in the National Cemeteries.*

Atlases

Andriot, Jay, comp. *Township Atlas of the United States.* McLean, Virginia: Documents Index, 1991. ◉

This is a single-volume edition of outline maps of and indexes to the minor county subdivisions of the 48 contiguous United States.

It contains a series of state maps showing the subdivisions of counties. Counties are divided into either Census County Divisions (CCD's) or Minor Civil Divisions (MCD's). Traditionally, census statistics have been presented for minor civil divisions for the entire country. This atlas provides maps to show the relative size and location within the county of either the Minor Civil Divisions or Census County Divisions.

The 48 individual state sections contain a state map and a corresponding county guide for locating each county within the state. It also has an individual state index which lists all subdivisions alphabetically under each county. The county maps show the Census County Divisions and/or the Minor Civil Divisions. State maps show the individual townships that resulted from the Public Land Survey.

The last portion of the book has a complete index which identifies all subdivisions, followed by the county and state in which each is located. Most, but not all locations listed in the Census Bureau publications are included in the index.

This is a handy reference source which gives convenient access to the township maps and information researchers need. It is an important tool for collections that serve research needs beyond the county.

Kansas Atlas and Gazetteer: Topographic Maps of the Entire State. Freeport, Maine: DeLorme, 1997. ISBN: 0-89933-215-3.

This is one of 36 atlases DeLorme has produced—one per state. They plan to produce one for every state in the United States. It is valuable for genealogical research because it is extremely detailed. Every library ought to have the one for their state, even if it is put in the general reference collection.

Rand, McNally and Co. ***Commercial Atlas and Marketing Guide.*** Chicago: Rand McNally, 1997. ISBN 0-528-8151-56.

This is a standard tool for most medium to large public libraries. Its also a good genealogy tool.

Catalogs

Filby, P. William. ***A Bibliography of American County Histories.*** Baltimore: Genealogical Publishing, 1985. ISBN 0-8063-1126-6.
A good reference tool for any serious library collection.

Kaminkow, Marion J., ed. ***A Complement to Genealogies in the Library of Congress: A Bibliography***. Baltimore: Magna Carta Book Co., 1981. ISBN: 0-910946-25-6.
This work has 20,000 family histories. A good bibliography for any reference collection.

————. ***U.S. Local Histories in the Library of Congress: A Bibliography.*** 5 vols. Baltimore: Magna Carta Book Co., 1975-76. ISBN 0-910946-17-5.
This five-volume set is a comprehensive bibliography of local histories through 1976.

Kemp, Thomas Jay, ***The 1995 Genealogy Annual: A Bibliography of Published Sources.*** Wilmington, Delaware: Scholarly Resources, 1996. ISBN: 0-8420-2661-4. ■
Primarily a bibliography of genealogical resources, this book is a helpful reference tool for librarians who want to build a basic genealogy collection. Annual updates are planned.

New England Historic Genealogical Society. Circulating Library. ***Circulating Library Catalog for the New England Historic Genealogical Society.*** 2 vols. 7th ed. Boston: New England Historic Genealogical Society, 1996.

Volume one lists over 5,724 family histories. Volume two contains 20,000 state and local histories.

Newberry Library, Chicago. ***The Genealogical Index.*** Boston: G.K. Hall, 1960. Microfilm. ISBN 0-8161-1317-3. 8 reels.

This is a massive work that is available for sale from the publisher. It is also available from Family History Library through Family History Centers. For very large collections only. (Microfilms 928135 through 928137)

U.S. Library of Congress. ***Genealogies Cataloged by the Library of Congress Since 1986: With a List of Established Forms of Family Names and a List of Genealogies Converted***

to Microfilm Since 1983. Washington, D.C.: Library of Congress, 1992. ✪
This catalog has 11,769 entries, and 3,564 titles on microfilm.

United States Local Histories in the Library of Congress: A Bibliography. Marion J. Kaminkow, ed. Baltimore: Genealogical Publishing, 1976. ISBN: 0-614-10566-8. ✪

This five-volume set is a condensation in book form of the 90,000 entries which form the shelflist of the Local History section of the Library of Congress. The first four volumes are arranged by geographic regions and include details on all local history books received by the Library of Congress up to 1972. The fifth volume is a supplement listing U.S. local histories received between 1972 and 1976.

University Microfilms International. *Family Histories for Genealogists: A Microfiche Program from UMI.* Ann Arbor: UMI, 1987. ∎

Periodicals

Staying Current
Reading genealogy magazines is one way to learn of new publications for your collection. Another way to request publishers catalogs. Check appendix B (p. 114) for a list of genealogical publishers.

Periodicals are important resources for genealogical research because they not only publish articles of current interest and research techniques, but they also publish the results of research which can provide genealogists with specific data they need. A one-page genealogy may be just the link someone needs to take their family tree back several generations, but to publish this short genealogy in book form would be financially infeasible. In this way, genealogical periodicals fill a special niche in the business of genealogical publishing.

A piece written by Desmond Walls Allen for *Heritage Quest* is a good example of the type of articles published in some of the genealogy periodicals. Entitled "World War I Draft Registration Records," the article is only a little over a thousand words long, but still a gem for any researcher who is searching for a male ancestor who might have been born in the U.S. between 1873 and 1900.

In her article on WWI draft registration, Allen discusses local draft boards and the legislation that set them up. She gives a list of the questions that were asked on the draft registration form and shows a facsimile of a completed one. All a researcher needs is the probable place of residence in 1917 and 1918. The article states:

> *This massive collection of draft registration cards, over 24 million, are housed at the National Archives—Southeast Region in East Point, Georgia. They have been filmed and are available through the Family History Library in Salt Lake City. Many libraries, archives and genealogical societies have purchased rolls of the microfilm specific to their area.*

The article goes on to give explicit directions on how to request a search from the National Archives. The article suggests ways to use the information gleaned from the record and recommends ways to follow-up on other leads. It concludes with a short bibliography of other places to look for more information. Articles like this help librarians and genealogists learn new research techniques.[1]

Periodical Indexes

The key to all the information in periodicals is an index. The most famous is *Periodical Source Index (PERSI)* compiled by the Allen County Public Library. It has recently become available in CD-ROM format.

PERSI: Periodical Source Index CD-ROM for Windows. Orem, UT: Ancestry, 1997.

The *Periodical Source Index*, or *PERSI*, is the largest index of genealogical and historical periodical articles in the world. This important research tool is a vital first link for any library.

PERSI is a comprehensive subject index to genealogy and local history periodicals written in English and French (Canadian) since 1800. The collection also includes literature dating from the 1700s, although the collection before 1800 is less complete. The Canadian section is remarkably complete. In printed form, *PERSI* spans 27 volumes and takes up several feet of shelf space.

PERSI contains more than one million fully searchable articles in almost 5,000 different periodicals. Articles are indexed according to locality, family (surname), and/or research method.

Once researchers find an article, a mouse click will take them to details about the article's publisher, publication date, and archive location. Using this information, they will be able to request copies of each article.

PERSI includes five major sections. Each article title in the database is accompanied by additional information about the name and date of the periodical where the article was printed along with a link to information about the publisher and sources for reprints. The major sections are: *Specific families (440,162 entries); Canada and Canadian peoples (21,510 entries); The United States and US peoples (547,650 entries); Lands and peoples outside the US and Canada (40,077 entries); Genealogy methods and skills (18,193 entries).*

Donald Lines Jacobus' *Index to Genealogical Periodicals*. Revised by Carl Boyer, 3rd. ed, Camden, Maine: Picton Press, 1995. (Reprinted August 1995 by Picton Press). ISBN: 0-897252-38-1.

This work is absolutely essential to researchers using genealogical and historical periodicals published between 1858 and 1952. Each volume has an alphabetically arranged name index, and a place and subject index. As a further aid to research, a valuable list of supplementary sources is included, such as the author's selective index of families treated in certain pedigree or ancestral books dealing chiefly with New England and New York families. This work is a useful tool for family history researchers, and belongs in research libraries. 3 vols. in 1.

Konrad, J. **Directory of Family "One-Name" Periodicals.** Munroe Falls, Ohio: Summit Publications. [Current year].

This serial publication gives the names and mailing addresses for approximately 2,000 newsletters in the United States and Canada. It also lists variant spellings and allied families. The work is very helpful in finding researchers on a particular surname.

General Genealogical Periodicals

Ancestry Magazine (Ancestry Inc., PO Box 990, Orem, UT 84059-0990). URL: http://www2.viaweb.com/ancestry/anmag.html *(Accessed 1/28/98)*

Informative and authoritative, this genealogical journal consistently provides articles from top-notch researchers and experts in the field. They stay on top of current topics and techniques.

Everton's Genealogical Helper (PO Box 368, Logan, UT 84321). URL: http://www.everton.com/about.html *(Accessed 1/28/98)*

The most widely read and used genealogical magazine in the world. Articles, advertisements, and classified ads help genealogists connect with each other.

FGS Forum (Federation of Genealogical Societies, PO Box 3385, Salt Lake City, UT 84110).
Has news and information of interest to genealogists and member societies.

Genealogical Computing (Ancestry Inc., PO Box 476, Salt Lake City, UT 84110-0476). URL: http://www2.viaweb.com/ancestry/gencom.html *(Accessed 1/30/98)*

The only genealogical magazine that offers in-depth coverage of technology issues for genealogists. Unites the newest in computer technology with time-honored pursuit of genealogy. Includes hands-on tips, software reviews and updates.

Genealogical Journal (PO Box 1144, Salt Lake City, UT 84110). URL: http://www.infouga.org/journal.htm *(Last updated 1/2/98) (Accessed 1/30/98)*

Articles and book reviews by professional researchers make it a valuable worldwide resource. Elaine Justesen, editor, welcomes unsolicited articles for the *Journal*, if they meet editorial guidelines.

Genealogy Bulletin (American Genealogical Lending Library, PO Box 329, Bountiful, UT 84011-0329). URL: http://www.agll.com/mag/genealogy_bulletin.html #about *(Accessed 1/30/98)*

This bulletin/newsletter publishes quality articles on genealogical research, news items, and the genealogical exchange includes approximately 3,000 surnames with information which will allow for contact between genealogists researching the same family name. Check out their Web site for sample articles. This publication belongs in every library and in the personal collection of most genealogists.

Heritage Quest Magazine (PO Box 329, Bountiful, UT 84011-0329). URL: http://www.heritagequest.com/ *(Accessed 1/30/98)*

An excellent reference tool for beginners and advanced researchers alike. Keeps up with technology for genealogists. Library news, periodical directory, tips for societies, library research technique articles, books, microforms, periodical reviews.

Life Story: The Family and Community Writer's Workshop (3591 Letter Rock Rd., Manhattan, KS 66502. Tel: 1-800-685-7330).

Most librarians may never come across this little magazine, but it is a real gem for anyone who wants to write their life story. Researchers who have spent years gathering their family history often like to see it produced as a book so they can share it with family members. This journal can help them attain this goal.

Mayflower Quarterly, A Journal of Family History in Colonial New England (General Society of Mayflower Descendants, PO Box 3297, Plymouth, MA 02361). URL: http://www.mayflower.org/ *(Accessed 1/30/98)*

Covers Pilgrim history, genealogy literature, and ads involving colonial New England.

National Genealogical Society Quarterly (PO Box 870212, University of Alabama, Tuscaloosa, AL 35487-0212). URL: http://www.genealogy.org/~ngs/ngsqtoc.html *(Last Updated 4/5/96) (Accessed 1/30/98)*

An academic/scholarly publication that features scholarly essays on methodology and resources for family history research. It has well-written, how-to-do-it articles on items of current interest.

New England Historical and Genealogical Register (101 Newbury St., Boston, MA 02116). URL: http://www.nehgs.org/index.htm *(Accessed 1/30/98)*

This is a quarterly journal of scholarly research that publishes family histories and genealogies of archival quality, with emphasis on New England families and their European origins. Subscription is free with membership in the New England Historical and Genealogical Society (NEHGS).

New York Genealogical and Biographical Record (122 E. 58th St., New York, NY 10022). URL: http://nygbs.org/Record.htm *(Updated 1/12/98) (Accessed 1/30/98)*

The *Record* is the second-oldest genealogical journal in the United States. It has a long history of scholarly articles written on genealogy, biography, and history relating to New York State. They include source material and compiled genealogies for New York State families.

Prologue: The Quarterly of the National Archives (NEPS-Room G-6, National Archives, Washington, D.C. 20408).

This list has historical articles retained in the holdings of the National Archives and Presidential Libraries.

Regional & State Genealogical Periodicals

American Genealogist (Box 398, Demorest, GA 30535-0398).

This academic/scholarly publication includes documented analyses of genealogical problems. Includes short compiled genealogies, generally in the southeastern U.S.

Connecticut Nutmegger (Connecticut Society of Genealogists Inc., PO Box 435, Glastonbury, CT 06033).

Publishes articles of original family research for Connecticut and New England. Includes book reviews, advertisements, Connecticut vital records, queries, Bible records, unpublished genealogies.

Illinois State Genealogical Society Quarterly (Illinois State Genealogical Society, PO Box 10195, Springfield, IL 62791). URL: http://smtp.tbox.com/isgs/SUBMTQRT.HTM *(Accessed 1/30/98)*

This quarterly publishes articles on Illinois settlers, genealogies, Illinois history, research aids and sources, computer genealogy, and offers free queries to members.

Hoosier Genealogist (Indiana Historical Society, 315 W. Ohio Street, Indianapolis, IN 46202-3299. Fax: 317/233-3109). URL:http://www.ihs1830.org/thg.htm *(Accessed 1/30/90)*

This is an academic and scholarly publication that prints original records of Indiana, including information on family Bibles, marriage, wills, court records and cemeteries.

Kentucky Ancestors (Kentucky Historical Society, Old State Capitol, PO Box 1792, Frankfort, KY 40602-1792). URL: http://www.state.ky.us/agencies/khs/research/ky_ancestors_query.htm *(Accessed 1/30/98)*

This is a family history publication featuring genealogical research and records from private and public sources throughout the state and the nation.

North Carolina Genealogical Society Journal (Box 1492, Raleigh NC 27602). URL: http://www.ncgenealogy.org/ *(Last edited 11/2/1997) (Accessed 1/30/98)*

This is a scholarly publication with articles of general genealogical value, including source data from original documents, and other material from previously unpublished sources.

Second Boat (Pentref Press, PO Box 2782, Kennebunkport, ME 04046-2782). URL: http://www.genealogyusa.com *(Accessed 1/30/98)*

This publication specializes in colonial American genealogy with an emphasis on pre-1650 immigrants and descendants on the East coast of North America. It publishes free queries on research before 1800.

Southern Queries (PO Box 23854, Columbia, SC 29224-3854). URL: http://www.mindspring.com/~freedom1/sq/sqmain.htm *(Last updated 1/3/98) (Accessed 1/30/98)*

This publication is for people researching ancestors and families in the South. Includes queries, how-to articles, calendar of family reunions, software reviews, and genealogical events.

Magazine of Virginia Genealogy (Virginia Genealogical Society, 5001 W. Broad St., Ste. 115, Richmond, VA 23230-3023). URL: http://www.vgs.org/magazine.htm *(Updated: 9/22/97) (Accessed 1/30/90)*

Provides primary source material for Virginia genealogy and oral history, with emphasis on eighteenth- and nineteenth-century vital statistics, court, and land records.

Other Periodicals For a listing of approximately 1,200 genealogical periodicals check: *Ulrich's International Periodicals Directory* (New Providence, NJ: R.R. Bowker, 1997. ISBN: 0-8352-3967-5).

Summary

Most libraries have a general materials selection policy. It should apply to the selection of materials for the genealogical collection, too. Better yet, it should contain a special section for local history and genealogy which should include collecting and preserving all available materials on local history. Some books that would be rejected for other parts of the collection because of format, binding, appearance, or content may be welcomed into the local history and genealogical collection because they are the only books available on the topic. There may be only one or two extant histories of your county. If another one is produced you shouldn't reject it because it doesn't have an index or is printed on a photocopier, or has a plastic comb binding. So if it is local history; keep it, regardless of its condition. Never weed a local history/genealogy book from the library. Even if it falls apart, put it in a plastic bag and keep it.

Criteria for Selection of Genealogical Books

If it is a genealogical resource, but is not local history, consider these evaluation criteria for books:

- Does it match selection criteria for the level of genealogical research you want your collection to provide? Is your library a regional or statewide resource? You will want to collect and preserve any materials pertaining to your region or state.

- Will the purchase of the material/book fit within the budget for the genealogical collection? Don't spend all of the local history budget at the beginning of the fiscal year. Something may come along later and you will need the money. Don't buy family histories unless they apply specifically to a family in the community. Acceptance of gifts from local citizens of family histories is appropriate. At least one family in the community has an interest. Others may, too.

- Does the book contain information that could be of value to your patrons? Don't buy or even collect books that have lists of names that have been copied from a telephone directory.

- Has the book been produced in a useable format? Does it have an index? Genealogical reference tools without indexes are not totally worthless, but they are sure difficult to use.

Notes

1. Allen, Desmond Walls, "World War I Draft Registration Records," *Heritage Quest: The Genealogy Magazine*. Number 71 (Sept./Oct. 1997) pp. 26-28.

Chapter 5

Libraries & Archives–Top 10

Survey of Libraries and Archives

As part of my research for this book I sent a short survey to about 250 libraries, archives, etc., to determine what support they provided for genealogical research. Many librarians and archivists responded, and I am grateful for their answers. After I compiled the responses, I checked out their Web sites. In some cases I was able to glean additional information from their home pages. Only a precious few make their materials available through interlibrary loan or loan materials directly to customers. Many research centers and archives will do varying amounts of research for out-of-town researchers who are unable to go their facilities. Their fees vary, but they seemed reasonable enough to me.

Trimming the list

By the time all of the responses came back and I started tabulating the results, I realized that I had more information than I could fit in this book. Besides that, there are already books on the market that list the libraries and archives and their addresses. For a library to be included here, it had to do more than say, "Here we are. If you want to use our genealogical collection, come to our library." Libraries that had very large or truly unique collections or offered some special service, even if that service is only accessible through their online catalog, made the list.

Top 10 List

The libraries and archives listed in this chapter are, in my opinion, exceptional and should be considered first when looking for information beyond your library and community. My are listed below.

1. The library has the quantity and quality of records that make it truly unique.

2. The library is physically accessible to researchers from more than one location, like the Family History Library and its Family History Centers or the National Archives and its regional centers. Others allow materials to go out through interlibrary loan.

3. The library has a catalog of its holdings that can be searched from a remote location such as a catalog on CD-ROM, a printed book catalog, or an online catalog available over the Internet.

4. The library has a significant number of records that actually contain the detailed information that genealogists need.

5. The library has special services such as professional researchers who will, for a fee, look up information for people who can't get to the site for research.

For a more extensive look at resource centers in the U.S. see *America's Best Genealogy Resource Centers* by William Dollarhide and Ronald A Bremer (Heritage Quest, 1998).

#1 Family History Library

35 N West Temple
Salt Lake City, UT 84150
Tel: 801-240-2331
Fax: 801-240-5551

The Family History Library and its network of branches or Family History Centers deserves to be at the top of this list not only because it is the largest genealogical research facility in the world, but also because Family History Centers across the U.S. and around the world make the resources of the Library available to people close to where they live. Its primary purpose is to provide members of The Church of Jesus Christ of Latter-day Saints with access to information so they can trace their ancestry.

The Family History Library will lend microfilm through its Family History Centers for a fee of $3.25 for 60 days. It does not lend books through its Family History Centers, but the Library will copy pages from the index of a book, and fill requests for copies of limited specific pages. A nominal charge applies.

The Collection

The Family History Library has over two million reels of microfilm—equivalent to about seven million 300-page volumes. They also have close to 400,000 microfiche—about 100,000 volumes, and over a quarter million books. The library adds about 100,000 rolls of microfilm each year.

Since the end of World War II, the Genealogical Society of Utah has been microfilming records throughout the world. Because of obvious storage and retrieval characteristics, microfilm continues to be the medium of choice for acquiring and maintaining genealogical records. About 30 years ago the Church started a coordinated plan to microfilm all available records in the U.S. They started in the eastern U.S. and are moving west. They are now microfilming records in eastern Kansas.

Bibliographic access to the collection is through the *Family History Library Catalog*. It is available in microfiche and CD-ROM format. The catalog on CD is part of *FamilySearch* and is available at all Family History Centers.

Format and type of records available   The collection is primarily microfilm of primary, secondary, and compiled records. If they have any original (primary source) documents, these are microfilmed and the film is put out for public use. The Library also has books and periodicals, many now located in the Joseph Smith Memorial Building.

On-Site Access

This library is open to the public for research free of charge. The only costs associated with using the Family History Library are those of making copies and printouts. The Library opens at 7:30 a.m. Monday through Saturday. It closes at 6:00 p.m. on Monday, at 10:00 p.m. from Tuesday through Friday, and at 5:00 p.m. on Saturday. The FHL is closed on the following holidays: New Year's Day, Memorial Day, Independence Day, Pioneer Day (July 24, a Utah state holiday), Labor Day, Thanksgiving Day, and Christmas Day.

Those who are planning to visit the FHL should consult the *Family History Library Catalog (FHLC)* in the nearest Family History Center before making the trip, printing out call numbers for the microfilms they wish to search.

The best thing about going to Salt Lake City is that you can search the contents of many, many films in one day at no charge. I have used more than 25 films in one day, and I'm sure that isn't even close to the record. There is usually no waiting to use a film. The patron can make photocopies of microfilm or books for a normal copy charge and take the copies home.

Professional staff

Another good thing about the FHL is the paid professional staff. Staff members are there to help people develop search strategies and suggest additional resources. These professionals have been extensively trained and have years of experience. They are not there to do research for individuals, but they are very approachable and helpful.

Hint
One clearly focused question from a researcher will help the professional staff member provide an answer that will give the patron a resource to check that could produce the desired result.

Patrons need to take their pedigree chart with them, just like we suggested in an earlier chapter. They need to focus on the one fact they want to find and not obscure the request with extraneous information.

Access from a Distance

The network of Family History Centers across the United States and around the world make the vast resources of the Family History Library more accessible than any other genealogical research center in the world. Except in sparsely populated areas, there is a Family History Center within a 20 to 40 minute drive for almost anyone who lives in the United States. The Church also has Centers in major population centers and near LDS Temples around the world.

The best way to find the nearest Family History Center is to look in the white pages of the local telephone directory under "Church of Jesus Christ of LDS." Call the number on Sunday and ask the person who answers where the nearest Family History Center is located. Then ask if they know the hours.[1]

Publications: *Research Outlines*

Family History Publications

To request the current *Family History Publication List* send your request to:

Salt Lake Distribution Center
1999 West 1700 South
Salt Lake City, UT 84104-4233

Using a credit card, individuals may order outlines for their own use by calling 1-800-537-5950.

The Family History Library has prepared *Research Outlines* which are available individually or as a set. In 52 pages or less, these outlines introduce strategies and describe content, uses and availability of major records for specific topics, states or regions. They have an outline for each state which sells for a dollar or less. The entire set for the U.S. can be purchased as a set for around $25. Prices and content change without notice, but the outlines are updated regularly.

Books about the Family History Library

The Library: A Guide to the LDS Family History Library. Cerny, Johni, and Wendy Elliot, eds. Salt Lake City: Ancestry Publishing, 1988. ISBN: 0-916489-21-3.

This is the most comprehensive book available on the Family History Center. It will give you a floor-by-floor summary of the collections and resources. Each chapter is written by a different specialist. The individual chapters focus on a specific geographic region of the U.S. or foreign regions and give an overview of the resources in the FHL for that region. There are useful lists and tables of important information.

This book belongs in every library because it has a comprehensive bibliography and is a good "next link." It is a must read for anyone planning a trip to Salt Lake City to do research.

Parker, J. Carlyle. *Going to Salt Lake City to Do Family History Research*. 3rd ed. Turlock, California: Marrietta Publishing, 1996. ISBN: 0-934153-14-0.

This book is much more than a guidebook to the Family History Library. It is also a basic guidebook for doing genealogical research. It outlines various strategies for preparing to use the resources of the Family History Library, including the development of a list of individuals the researcher would like to find out more about. It describes how to prepare for a visit to the library by using the resources of a local Family History Center. And finally, it describes how to use the resources in the Library.

#2 National Archives and Records Administration (NARA)

700 Pennsylvania Ave., NW
Washington, DC 20408
Tel: 202/501-5400

The National Archives (NARA) has the backing of the federal government and a constitutional mandate to preserve the records of our country. Its broad powers and vast resources has allowed it to build a network of research facilities and amass a collection that is second to none. NARA has printed catalogs of all its microfilm and films that are readily available to individuals and other institutions. For an institution this large, the National Archives epitomizes accessibility. The agency rivals the Family

History Library in attracting genealogists.

Although the principle purpose of the National Archives is not that of helping genealogists find their ancestors, the documents they have collected and preserved contain so much information genealogists need, that we cannot overlook the research value of these records.

The following information is a summary of what you can find at the NARA Web site (http://www.nara.gov/nara/vision/vision.html). *(Updated 10/16/97) (Accessed 1/30/98)*

The Collection

Most used of the National Archives' collections are the federal censuses. They have all the censuses from 1790–1920 (accept for 1890) on microfilm. Other records include: Military Service Records, Immigrant and Passenger Arrivals Genealogical and Biographical Research, Federal Court Records, American Indians, and Black Studies.

Format and type of records available Primary source documents. These documents have been microfilmed and are available for purchase or rental.

On-Site Access

Going to the National Archives in Washington, DC, is the best way to get access to the collection. Genealogists make up the lion's share of researchers who use the Archives. Not only do they have a major research facility with several reading rooms in the Washington area, but they also have thirteen regional records service facilities strategically located around the country. While they are constantly working to make their records available electronically, it will be many years before a significant portion of their genealogical records will be online. In the interim, they have prepared finding aids, guides, and research tools to prepare researchers for a visit to one of their facilities.

Access from a Distance

If you can't get to Washington for access to these resources, try getting to one of the thirteen regional sites (see appendix A p. 113). For most people a trip to one of the regional archives is a day trip. If you can't get to one of the regional sites, you can use what is available on the Internet and rent films directly from NARA.

Genealogical resources on the World Wide Web

You may want to check out the NARA site: www.nara.gov/genealogy/genindex.html.

Also, NAIL, the Archives' online search engine, is worth looking at for a sample of their online information (www.nara.gov/nara/nail/searchnail.html). I helped a genealogist in one of my classes find his Native American ancestors who had been enrolled in one of the Cherokee tribes in this way.

Microfilm rental program

The National Archives will rent microfilm to individuals. They claim the lowest prices around—as low as $2.25 a roll (if you rent 10 films at a time), and they promise the best clarity and readability available. Films rent for a full 30 days. Individuals can rent official microfilm rolls by becoming a member of the National Archives Rental Program or they can order films through their local libraries.

The membership fee is $25. New members receive a *Start-up Kit* that contains everything researchers need to begin using the archives resources.

Using the local library to access the National Archives

If your library isn't one of the more than 6,000 libraries nationwide that participate in the National Archives Microfilm Rental Program, find out what you need to do to offer this service to your patrons. Call 301-604-3699.

Publications

Here is a list of publications for genealogists: *Beginning Your Genealogical Research, How to Use NARA's Census Microfilm Catalogs, Naturalization Records, The Soundex Indexing System, Post Office Records.*

NARA, Washington
Research hours for the Washington facility are:

Monday & Wednesday
    8:45 am - 5:00 p.m.
Tuesday, Thursday & Friday
    8:45 am - 9:00 p.m.
Saturday
    8:45 am - 4:45 p.m.
Closed Sunday

To Order Microfilm
If you need more information on how to order microfilm, contact:
Publications Distribution NECD
National Archives, Room G9
7th and Pennsylvania Ave., NW
Washington, DC 20408

Books about the National Archives

Greene, Evarts B., and Virginia D. Harrington. *American Population Before the Federal Census of 1790.* Baltimore: Genealogical Publishing. Reprint 1993. ✪

United States. National Archives and Records Administration. *Guide to Federal Records in the National Archives of the United States.* Washington, DC: National Archives and Records Administration, 1995. 3 vols. (For sale by the U.S. G.P.O., Supt. of Docs. NO: AE 1.108:G 94/V.1-3) ISBN: 0-160483-1-23. ◉

This supersedes both the 1974 edition and the 1987 reprint. It includes descriptions of federal records in the National Archives of the United States as of September 1, 1994.

Szucs, Loretto Dennis, and Sandra Hargreaves Luebking. *The Archives: A Guide to the National Archives Field Branches.* Salt Lake City: Ancestry, Inc. 1988. ◉

#3 National Genealogical Society

4527 17th St.
Arlington, VA 22207-2399
Tel: 703/525-0050 ext. 331
Toll Free: 800/473-0060
Fax: 703/525-0052
Email: library@ngsgenealogy.org
URL:
http://www.genealogy.org/~ngs/
(Accessed 1/30/98)
Online catalog:
http://206.239.149.67/ *(Accessed 1/30/98)*

The National Genealogical Society is the premier national membership organization for genealogists. Since 1903 it has been assisting its members trace their family histories. It provides leadership and education for individuals, societies, and institutions through programs, publications, and service to over 15,000 members. This library made it into my top five list because they circulate materials through the mail for the cost of postage. The loan service is available to members on-site or through the mail.

The Society collects, preserves, and disseminates genealogical information and source materials and provides education and training in genealogical research. The NGS encourages excellence in genealogical writing and serves as a nucleus for family research at the national level.

This is a membership organization with basic dues of $40 per year. This seems reasonable to me, especially in light of the benefits members enjoy. Most genealogical societies have a publication that is included with the membership benefits, but if they have a library or research facilities members have to travel to the location of the library to take advantage of library services. The lending service to members makes the National Genealogical Society unique. They also offer member discounts for enrollment for training seminars and home study courses.

Another valuable benefit is the Members' Ancestor Charts (MAC) File. This unique collection is designed to help members contact other members interested in the same families. New members are asked, as a contribution to the society, to complete, as far as possible, a chart for each of their four great-grandfathers. These charts on three generations, including the parents and children of each of their great-grandfathers are made a permanent NGS record. Since 1969, approximately a million names with their vital statistics have been submitted. Members are encouraged to file as many other charts pertaining to their ancestors as they wish. Members may request up to four surname searches at one time. There is no charge for this service.

The Collection

The Society's 30,000 volume private library in Arlington, Virginia, maintains a collection of family and local histories, genealogies, transcribed source materials, reference works, periodicals, Bible records, and manuscripts.

Format and type of records available Primarily printed materials (books and periodicals), though they also have some primary source documents like Bible records and manuscripts. Most of what they have are compiled records.

On-Site Access

This private library is open to members; non-members pay $5 per day.

Access from a Distance

The NGS Library does not lend through interlibrary loan. The Society provides a research service for members who cannot visit the library in person. A small group of experienced volunteers search the Library collection for members who cannot come to the library. Most searches focus on one individual, but some are directed to particular books or microfiche. Research is conducted at the rate of $15 per hour and involves anywhere from one to six hours of volunteer time. They charge individuals and libraries for copies at 25¢ per page plus $1.50.

The National Genealogical Society has acquired the American Medical Association's cardfile of deceased American physicians, amounting to some 350,000 records. The cards provide birth and death information for physicians who died between 1906 and 1964. For a fee they will search the card file and send a report. In most cases they can find the record knowing no more than the name of the physician. Call 1-800-4573-0060 ext. 331.

Publications

National Genealogical Newsletter   The bimonthly *NGS Newsletter* features articles about genealogy as well as news of the Society. Regular features of the newsletter include: Queries from members, Highlights of member genealogical activities, Reports reunion announcements from Family Societies, Advertisements for materials and services. Articles are solicited from all members.

The *NGS/CIG Digest* features information of interest to persons who use computers in researching or recording their genealogical information. Articles cover the use of specific genealogical software, the Internet and the genealogical materials located there—including the NGS home page.

National Genealogical Society Quarterly   Published since 1912, the *National Quarterly* has included material concerning all regions of the nation and all ethnic groups—including compiled genealogies, case studies, essays on new methodology and little-known resources, critical reviews of current books, and previously unpublished source materials. The *NGS Quarterly* captures the challenge of modern genealogy and proves that the best-done research is never boring.

The *Quarterly* is available on microfiche. (Hard copy sets are no longer available). The 1912–1994 issues of the *NGS Quarterly* on microfiche are sold as one set only. The 1995 issues and all issues after that date on microfiche are sold in one-year increments. The price to members for the 1912–1994 set is more than $100 off.

The *NGS Quarterly* emphasizes scholarship, readability and practical help in genealogical problem solving. Published in March, June, September, and December, each issue contains 80 pages. Articles show how to cope with name changes, burned courthouses, illegitimacies, and other stumbling blocks; how to interpret records that do not mean what they seem to say; how to distinguish between individuals of the same name; how to identify origins of immigrant ancestors; how to research a variety of ethnic groups; how to find a way through the maze of records at the National Archives; how to conduct research in specific states; and how to compile good genealogies.

All members receive the *Quarterly*. Manuscripts and correspondence regarding the *Quarterly* should be sent to: Editor, *NGS Quarterly*, 4527 17th Street North, Arlington, Virginia 22207-2399.

#4 New York Public Library

Fifth Ave. and 42nd St.
New York, NY 10018
Tel: 212-930-0828
Email: histref@nypl.org
URL: www.nypl.org
Online catalog:
www.nypl.org/catalogs/
  catalogs.html

The U.S. History, Local History and Genealogy Division of the New York Public Library is a major research center with 300,000+ volumes, 112,000 photos, 417,000 postcards. Interlibrary loan is free to reciprocal libraries. Up to ten photocopies are free to reciprocal libraries. Printed catalogs may be available in many research libraries. This collection is in my top ten because of its incomparable collection and the fact that the library will lend at least some of its materials to other libraries.

The Collection

The genealogical research collection includes many unique resources. Since the stacks are closed, researchers have to rely on their catalogs to identify the materials they want to use. Many of these research tools have been compiled from original records and will contain the type of data genealogists are seeking.

New York City Vital Records Indexes These indexes enable researchers to acquire copies of vital records from the New York City Municipal Archives and Department of Health. The indexes themselves must be used on site. Indexes available: *Index to Births, 1888-1982; Index to Deaths, 1888-1982; Index to Marriages, 1888-1937.*

Passenger Lists and Indexes The Library acquires published passenger lists and indexes, including those available through the National Archives on microfilm: Federal census records and extant Soundex indexes are available on microfilm in the Center for the Humanities for: *New York, New Jersey, Connecticut, 1790-1880; New York 1900; New York, New Jersey, Conn., Puerto Rico, 1910; New York, Puerto Rico, 1920.*

New York State Census The following state census records are available: *New York County, 1855 and 1905 (includes Bronx), 1915, 1925; Bronx County, 1915, 1925; Kings County, 1915, 1925; Queens County, 1915, 1925; Richmond County, 1865/75, 1915, 1925; Nassau County, 1915, 1925; Suffolk County, 1915, 1925; Westchester County, 1905, 1915, 1925.*

Regional Records The Division has a copy of the vast Barbour Collection of Connecticut Vital Records to 1850, and the Massachusetts Vital Records Microfiche Series.

Newspapers and Indexes The Library has an extensive collection of newspapers, however, there are few indexes to their contents. Among the available indexes are: *The New York Times Obituaries Index: 1858-1978; New York, New York Times, 1970-80; Personal Name Index to The New York Times Index, 1851-1989. 34 v.; Deaths taken from the Brooklyn Eagle, 1841-1880; Marriages taken from the Brooklyn Eagle, 1841-1880; New York Evening Post: Deaths, 1801-1890; New York Evening Post: Marriages, 1801-1890.*

Family Histories The Library's large collection of family histories, acquired by purchase and gifts, are accessed in the catalogs under the standard form of the family's surname. These compiled records are often rich in family anecdotes and genealogical data.

Format and type of records available The collections consist mostly of printed materials (books and periodicals) though some of their vital records and indexes are compiled from original documents.

On-Site Access

Patrons must rely on the catalogs because most library materials are held in closed stacks. The 18-volume printed catalog of the Division is arranged by author, subject and sometimes title, and includes materials acquired and cataloged from the date of founding of the Library through 1971. For works acquired after 1971, patrons use CATNYP, the Library's online computer catalog.

Access from a Distance

The Library will lend some of its materials on interlibrary loan to reciprocal libraries. The online catalog is now available over the Internet at nyplgate.nypl.org; login nypl (lower case). Internet access gives patrons across the country access to this vast collection.

#5 Library of Congress

Local History and Genealogy
  Reading Rm.
Jefferson Bldg, Rm LJ G42
Washington, DC 20540
Email: lcweb@loc.gov
URL: http://lcweb.loc.gov/rr/
genealogy/lhg.html
Online Catalog:
http://lcweb.loc.gov/catalog/
Accessed (1/30/98)

The Library of Congress has one of the world's premier collections of U.S. and foreign genealogical and local historical publications. The Library's genealogy collection began as early as 1815 when Thomas Jefferson's library was purchased. They made the top ten list in spite of the fact that you must go there to use the collection. Serious genealogists spend weeks, even months using this library.

The Collection

Printed materials, primarily books, are the main strength of the Library's Local History and Genealogy Reading Room. The Library has more than 40,000 genealogies and 100,000 local histories. The collections are especially strong in North American, British Isles, and German sources. While the Library's collection is strong in manuscripts, microfilms, newspapers, photographs, maps, and published material, it is not an archive or repository for unpublished or primary source materials.

Format and type of records available Primarily books and compiled records—*but what a collection.*

On-Site Access

You really have to go there to use the collection. You begin by registering for a photo identification card which allows you to request books to use in the library. It takes about an hour for the staff to retrieve requested materials. I found that their online catalog has the more recent publications and the card catalog, which has been closed for more than ten years, covers the older materials.

Access from a Distance

Users can access the catalog through the Web site to identify holdings, but there are no provisions for remote access to the collection.

Books About the Library of Congress

Neagles, James C. *The Library of Congress: A Guide to Genealogical and Historical Research.* Salt Lake City: Ancestry, 1990. ISBN: 0-916489-484. ◉

This is a comprehensive guide to The Library of Congress. It is a must read for anyone who plans to go there for genealogical research. With maps and full descriptions of the collections, this book says it all.

#6 Allen County Public Library

Reynolds Historical Genealogy
  Dept.
900 Webster St.
PO Box 2270
Fort Wayne, IN 46801-2270
Tel: 219/421-1225
Direct: 214/424-1330
Fax: 219/422-9688
URL: http://www.acpl.lib.in.us
Online Catalog:
http://www.acpl.lib.in.us/
  Genealogy/genealogy.html
(Accessed 1/30/98)

The Historical Genealogy Department made it into the top ten because their tremendous financial commitment to genealogists, their online public access catalog, and their unsurpassed periodical collection.

The Collection

The department's renowned collection contains more than 220,000 printed volumes and 260,000 items of microfilm and microfiche. The collection expands daily. While they have many microfilms of original records, most of what they have are compiled records, either from original sources or compiled from many sources. Here is a brief summary of their holdings taken from their brochure.

Family Histories: The collection claims more than 38,000 vols. of compiled genealogies representing research already done on American and European families. Nearly 5,000 genealogies on microfiche and numerous family newsletters round out this collection.

Census Records: ACPL is one of very few public libraries to have all of the *Federal Census Population Schedules* from 1790–1920. This collection can be accessed through all available statewide indexes and soundexes which are also in the library. They also have all extant mortality schedules for 1850–1880; all extant schedules of Civil War Union veterans and widows through 1890; and the Agricultural and Manufacturing schedules for Indiana for 1850–1880.

State and territorial census on microfilm are available for California, Colorado, Florida, Illinois, Iowa, Kansas, Michigan, Minnesota, Mississippi, Missouri, Nebraska, New Jersey, New Mexico, New York, Oregon, Rhode Island, Washington, and Wisconsin. Coverage varies by year and state.

City Directories: The department has a depository collection of 30,000 R.L. Polk directories dated from 1964 to the present. The department also holds many directories for smaller cities and rural areas produced by other publishers. The collection also includes city directories currently being micropublished by Research Publications of America. Coverage for U.S. cities includes: 1785-1860 microfiche (240 cities); 1861-1935 microfilm (79 cities); 1964–present (Polk directories).

Passenger Lists: Most National Archives passenger lists and indexes are available on microfilm. So are most of the major printed sources of immigration records.

Indexes include Filby's *Passenger and Immigration Lists Index; Famine Immigrants: Lists of Irish Immigrants arriving at...New York 1846–1851* (Detroit: Gale Research); *German Immigrants from Bremen to New York 1847–1867* (by Gary J. Zimmerman & Marion Wolfert, Baltimore: Genealogical Publishing); and *Germans to America 1850–1893* (in progress).

Military Records Holdings include most microfilmed National Archives service and pension records covering every conflict from the Revolutionary War through the Philippine Insurrection. Civil War regimental histories are on microfiche. Significant Confederate records from state archives are also available on microfilm.

U.S. Local Records Nearly 100,000 printed volumes are testimony to the department's efforts to comprehensively collect U.S. genealogy and local history publications. All the standard reference works are here, including *The American Genealogical-Biographical Index* and the *National Union Catalog of Manuscript Collections.* County and town histories, vital, cemetery, church, court, land, probate and naturalization records can all be accessed through department catalogs.

The Department also has significant collections for Canada, the British Isles, and Germany. Resources are also available to aid in locating African American and Native American records.

Periodicals ACPL holds the largest English-language genealogy and local history periodical collection in the world with more than 3,200 current subscriptions and more than 4,100 titles. Individual articles may be accessed through a variety of indexes including the *PERiodical Source Index (PERSI)*, compiled by department staff. (See p.52 for more information about *PERSI*.)

Format and type of records available Mostly compiled printed resources (books and periodicals) , but they also have all of the census films available from the National Archives.

Library hours:
Mon.–Thurs. 9 a.m. to 9 p.m.
Friday-Saturday 9 a.m. to 6 p.m.
Sunday 1 p.m. to 6 p.m.
(Closed on Sundays, Memorial
Day weekend thru Labor Day).

On-Site Access

The collection is not available on interlibrary loan. While some photocopying service is available for a fee, the best way to access the collection is to go there and use it in person. The Department is so large you will need their free map. Then watch the orientation video. Librarians experienced in genealogical research are always on duty to answer questions. Groups should notify the Department in advance.

Access from a Distance

Interlibrary loan is not an option, but they will photocopy pages from their extensive periodical collection. Use *PERiodical Source Index (PERSI)* (see page ??) Request their form for requesting photocopies of articles. They charge $1.50 per sheet of periodical requests plus 20 cents a page for photocopies.

#7   New England Historic and Genealogical Society

101 Newbury St.
Boston, MA 02116
Tel: 617/536-5740
Fax: 617/536-7307
Email: mtaylor@neghs.org
URL: http://www.nehgs.org/
(Updated on 11/15/97)
(Accessed 1/30/98)

If your genealogical research leads to the New England, this is the best research facility around. The library of New England Historic and Genealogical Society is a major genealogical repository. It is open to the public, but is funded with private funds and membership fees. Non-members pay a fee to use it. Members can use the circulating collection for a fee. Photocopies are also available for a fee.

The Collection

While the primary focus of the collection is New England, it also has materials for the entire United States, Canada, the British Isles, Ireland, and continental Europe. The Canadian collection is especially impressive. The Manuscript and Rare Books section has over a mile of unpublished manuscripts, genealogies, and books. Since the 1850s, NEGHS has been the repository for the works of principal genealogists in America. Over 200,000 books, one million microforms, plus a rapidly growing collection of CD-ROMs are available for on-site use.

Format and type of records available Extensive manuscript holdings, but primarily printed (compiled) materials and microfilms of original records.

On-Site Access

Members enjoy unlimited on-site use of the NEHGS Research Library, including access to the rare book and manuscript collections, and consultations with genealogical reference staff. In the Manuscript and Rare Book collections the stacks are closed and staff members retrieve materials from call slips. Manuscripts and rare books can be photocopied at the discretion of the librarian on duty.

    Non-members may use the main collection for a fee. My advice: If you are going to spend the money to travel to Boston to use this library, spend the money to become a member, too. Take the time to read the membership information or check out their Web site before making a trip to the library.

Queries should be sent to:
Enquiries Service
C/O NEHGS
101 Newbury St.
Boston, MA 02116
Fax: 617-536-7307

Access from a Distance

Members can borrow (rent) books from the 25,000 volume Circulating Library by mail. They have several skilled genealogists who will, for a fee, do research in the NEHGS library. This service was established to meet the demand for competent research in the New England area and elsewhere.

    They will only accept mail or fax requests. They ask people to write clearly and concisely, to provide all the information gathered so far, including citations for sources. They also ask questioners to specify the number of hours authorized to work on the project, and to send pre-payment for services, excluding expenses which will be billed later.

Publications

Membership includes a subscription to *The New England Historical and Genealogical Register*, which is one of the leading genealogical periodicals in the world.

#8 Daughters of the American Revolution

1776 D St., NW
Washington, D.C. 20006-5392
Tel: 202-879-3229
Fax: 202-879-3227
URL: www.dar.org

The DAR is one of the nation's premier genealogical research centers. Incorporated by an act of Congress in 1896, the NSDAR is a nonprofit, non-political, volunteer service organization with nearly 180,000 members in some 3,000 chapters. The Society was founded in Washington, DC, in 1890 and has celebrated more than one hundred years of service through historic preservation, promotion of education and patriotism.

The Collection

The DAR has 150,000 volumes; 250,000 files; and 40,000 microforms. It is privately funded and open to members free; non-members pay a daily fee. Most of the printed materials are in open stacks and organized by family surname or geographic regions, broken down to counties and then cities.

Format and type of records available Mostly printed compiled documents (books and periodicals), good microfilm collection.

The library is open to the public
Monday–Friday
  8:45 a.m. – 4 p.m.
Sunday
  1 p.m. – 5 p.m.
  except holiday weekends.

Unannounced closings may occur. Please check before planning a visit from a distance.

On-Site Access

Non-members pay a $5 daily fee—a bargain for access to such a vast collection. The online catalog is very useful, especially with surname research. But browsing the stacks in the geographic section is also an effective way to find materials. Staff members make requested photocopies for 20¢ a page.

Access from a Distance

Orders for photocopies by mail must come to the Library's research service directly from the researcher. Telephone assistance is available for very specific questions and general information. Non-members pay a flat fee of $10 for up five pages. Non-members pay $25 per hour for research.

#9 Mid-Continent Public Library

Genealogy & Local History Dept.
Mid-Continent Public Library
317 West 24 Hwy.
Independence, MO
Tel: 816-252-0950
Fax: 816-252-6364
Email: ge@mcpl.lib.mo.us
URL: http://www.mcpl.lib.mo.us

The Mid-Continent Public Library made into my top ten list because they have a circulating collection they lend to the public free and on interlibrary loan. They also have a tremendous online catalog. They only lend microfilm to Missouri libraries.

The Collection

The collection consists mainly of books. Also worth noting is their collection of the UMI Genealogy and Local History Series on microfiche. The Circulating Collection began in 1984 with a small set of books donated to the Library by the American Family Records Association [AFRA]. Kermit Karns, then President of AFRA, envisioned a genealogy collection available to researchers nationwide through local public libraries. The collection has grown to almost 5,000 volumes. Last year the Library lent 3,612 books to researchers in 43 states and Canada.

Format and type of records available Mostly printed compiled documents (books and periodicals), good microfilm and microfiche collection.

On-Site Access

Anyone can walk in and use the collection. They have professional librarians on duty to help with reference questions. The online catalog is user friendly and will lead the researcher easily to the documents needed. They have printed catalogs and supplements available, and their online catalog is available at:

http://www.mcpl.lib.mo.us/disclaim.htm. *(Accessed 1/30/98)*

Access from a Distance

Over 5,000 genealogy and local history books available are on interlibrary loan to researchers nationwide. Interested individuals should write for a free copy of *Genealogy from the Heartland, A Catalog of Titles in the Mid-Continent Public Library Genealogy Circulation Collection* (1992-1994 Supplement, 1996 Supplement). This catalog lists the books available on loan through local public libraries. The 1994 and 1996 supplements may be downloaded from the Web page.

The staff does not conduct extensive genealogical research, but they will check indexed materials as time permits. Requests may be submitted by telephone, email, and regular mail. There is no charge for these services, but donations are always appreciated. Photocopy charges, 15¢ per page. Invoices for copy charges will be sent with copied materials. The library has a list of local researchers who will do research for a fee.

#10 Heritage Quest

593 West. 100 North
PO Box 329
Bountiful, UT 84011-0329
Tel: 801-298-5358
Fax: 801-298-5468
Email: sales@heritagequest.com
URL: http://www.heritagequest.
  com/ (Accessed 1/30/98)

Heritage Quest is a genealogical resource company that specializes in renting microfilm and microfiche. They made it on my top ten list despite the fact that they are a commercial provider. Their membership fee ($39) is comparable to the membership of the National Genealogical Society and other genealogical societies. They are able to make a lot of resources available to their members because they have more privately held microfilm than any other organization in America. To make some microfilm more readable, Heritage Quest has enhanced the images of National Archives census microfilm. If you have tried to read some of the census film produced by the archives, you will know this enhancement makes their collection of census film exceptional.

The Collection

The collection is fully accessible by Heritage Quest members on loan with over 250,000 microfilm and microfiche titles related directly to genealogy subjects. These include copies of all of the microfilm produced by the National Archives. The topics covered by the microform catalog include: *Census Records 1790-1920; Military Records; Selected State Censuses; Surname Collections; Ship Passenger Lists; Vital Records; County Records; Indexes; African American Records; Native American Records; Special Collections; County, Local, and Family Histories.*

Format and type of records available Exclusively microfilm, microfiche of original and secondary documents.

On-Site Access

None. Members and customers can walk in and buy books, materials and films. With the Family History Library just ten miles away the people at Heritage Quest feel that facilities for on-site research would be superfluous.

Access from a Distance

This is what Heritage Quest does best. They rent microfilm or microfiche for $3.25 per roll of film or fiche title. Their catalog is available free to personal members and for sale to institutions that want to rent or buy films for their patrons. Visit their Web site for more information about their services.

Publications

They publish two well-respected genealogical magazines: *Heritage Quest* and *The Genealogy Bulletin.*

Notes
1. Dollarhide, William, "All Roads Lead to Salt Lake City: Preparing for and Visiting The Family History Library." *Genealogy Bulletin,* 29 (Sept./Oct. 1995) pp.1–17.)

Chapter 6

Libraries & Archives– Significant Collections

*T*he libraries here made the main list because they qualified on some, but not all, of the elements of the top ten list (p. 57). Many of the state archives offered some form of research and a photocopy service. It is probably a good idea to ask about current charges before requesting services.

If you want to find libraries with genealogical collections not included in this book, check *The Genealogist's Address Book* by Elizabeth Bentley (Genealogical Publishing, 1998.) or *Subject Collections* compiled by Lee Ash (Bowker). Both books have long lists of libraries that have significant genealogical collections.

Another good resource is *America's Best Genealogy Resource Centers* by Ronald Bremer and William Dollarhide. This book identifies the best genealogical research facilities at local, state, regional, and national levels. The authors are two of the most traveled genealogists in America. They have visited all of the centers described in this book. While visiting each facility, they asked staff about their special collections, surname folder files, genealogies, periodicals, county histories, and any other genealogical resources. The original list of 3,000 was condensed to an elite group of about 600 facilities. This is an indispensable tool for librarians who help their patrons locate genealogical information in other facilities.

Planning a Trip to a Major Research Facility

The collections of the research facilities on this list are significant. For many genealogists visiting one or more of them could be worth the effort. Here are some suggested things to do before making the trip to any library or distant facility for research.

- Get access to library's catalog and look up materials you want to search before making the trip. You could use their online catalog over the Internet or the *Family History Library Catalog* on CD-ROM for the Family History Library in Salt Lake City.
- Conduct a place search to find out what is available in the area of your research.
- Conduct a surname search to learn if any records are available on your family names.
- Compile a check list of ancestors you want to find.
- Prepare note cards that include what you already have and suggest places to look for more information.

List of Libraries and Genealogical Research facilities

The libraries on the following list represent a commitment of service to family history researchers. If they will lend at least some of their materials through interlibrary loan I have indicated that service with "ILL-Yes" at the end of the address information. I have organized them by state into six broad categories: (1) Public Libraries, (2) State Libraries and Archives, (3) Historical Societies, (4) Academic Libraries, (5) Commercial Libraries, (6) Special Libraries/Archives.

In some cases there is an overlap. Some state historical societies are the state archives. Some are not.

Public Libraries

Colorado

Denver Public Library
Western History/Genealogy, 10 W. 14th Ave. Pkwy., Denver, CO 80204-2749
Tel: 303-640-6291. Fax: 303-640-6298
URL: http://denver.lib.co.us/ *(Accessed 1/30/98)*

This is the local history and genealogical section of a major public library with 60,000 volumes and 75,000 microforms. Access is free and open to the public. Up to ten copies are free to other libraries via ILL. Individuals pay a minimum of $1, (10¢ per page) when they write direct.

Florida

Indian River County Main Library
Florida History and Genealogy Dept., 1600 21st St., Vero Beach, FL 32960
Tel: 561-770-5060. Fax: 561-770-5066. Email: phal@iu.net
URL: http://www.rootsweb.com/~flindian/ircl/ *(Updated 11/26/97) (Accessed 1/30/98)*

The Indian River County Main Library, Florida History and Genealogy Department offers 35 reasons to visit the library for genealogical research. They include: Three computers that provide access to almost one hundred CD-ROMs for genealogical research, complete federal census records for 1790–1860, *FamilySearch*, Civil War books, and an extensive collection of indexes and compiled records on microfiche and microfilm. All interlibrary loan and mail requests should be specific, give exact dates, names and locations. A copy of a pedigree chart is not required but would be appreciated. Extensive research will not be done. Phone requests for research are not accepted. The minimum charge is $2 which includes five photocopies. Additional copies are 10¢ per page. Photocopies of microfilm are 25¢ per page. Send a self-addressed stamped envelope. Make the check payable to Indian River County Main Library.

Georgia

Atlanta-Fulton Public Library System (AFPL)
Genealogy & Georgia History Dept., One Margaret Mitchell Sq., Atlanta, GA 30303
Tel: 404-730-1940. Fax: 404-730-1731. (No reference questions by fax.)
URL: http://www.af.public.lib.ga.us *(Updated 1/26/98) (Accessed 1/30/98)*

AFPL has 17,000+ volumes, 31,000+ microforms, 556 vertical files, and 3,069 maps. Access to the collection is free and open to the public, although no genealogical materials circulate. Librarians should consult OCLC for the most updated statement of the ILL department's policies. The department staff can photocopy up to twelve pages in response to clearly described requests. The first four pages are free; all thereafter are 15¢ each.

Indiana

Monroe County Public Library
Indiana Rm., 303 East Kirkwood Ave., Bloomington, IN 47408
Tel: 812-349-3080. Email: Through Web site.
URL: http://www.monroe.lib.in.us *(Accessed 1/30/98)*

This public library has approximately 2,000 titles in their genealogical collection, some of which they will lend on interlibrary loan. They will gladly copy materials for out-of-state patrons. Send a self-addressed stamped envelope with the request and enough money to cover the cost of copying at 10¢ per page. The first three pages are free.

Vigo County Public Library
One Library Sq., Terre Haute, IN 47807
Tel: 812-232-1113. Fax: 812-232-3208
URL: http://vax1.vigo.lib.in.us/ *(Accessed 1/30/98)*

Researchers may contact the library directly without going through their local libraries. Copying charge to individuals is 15¢ per page, plus postage. Staff members respond to queries received by mail, telephone, fax, or email. Queries are answered in the order they are received, so the length of time for reply may vary. Only a limited amount of time may be devoted to each request. There is no charge for research.

Kansas

Iola Public Library
218 E. Madison, Iola, KS 66749
Tel: 316-365-3262. Fax: 316-365-5137. Email: rogerc@midusa.net
URL: http://skyways.lib.ks.us/kansas/library/iola/INDEX.HTML *(Accessed 1/30/98)*.
Online catalog: http://skyways.lib.ks.us/kansas/sekls/genealogy/pdf/index.html (PDF Format)
(Updated 9.14/97) (Accessed (1/30/98)
ILL: Free in Kansas, charge to out-of-state libraries.

This is a small public library with a good genealogical collection, including 2,300 volumes and 8,000 rolls of microfilm available on interlibrary loan. Walk-in borrowers can obtain materials free of charge. ILL for Kansas libraries is free, but they charge out-of-state libraries. Their printed catalog sells for $40. Up to ten photocopies are free to other libraries.

Louisiana

New Orleans Public Library
Louisiana Div., 219 Loyola Ave., New Orleans, LA 70112-2049
Tel: 504-596-2610. Fax: 504-596-2609. Email: nopl@gnofn.org
URL: http://www.gnofn.org/~nopl/guides/genguide/ggcover.htm *(Accessed 1/30/98)*

The Louisiana Division is the official City Archives of New Orleans. It is also the official repository of the pre-1928 records of the Civil Courts and the pre-1932 records of the Criminal Courts of Orleans Parish. Photocopies of specific pages in books, periodicals, and microfilms can be made by the Division at a cost of $2 per page. Send a self-addressed stamped envelope with the request. Limited search services are available for a fee. Contact the Louisiana Division for details.

Shreve Memorial Library
424 Texas, P.O. Box 21523, Shreveport, LA 71120-1523
Tel: 318-226-5890. Fax: 318-226-4780. Email: cliggins@smlnet.sml.lib.la.us
URL: http://www.prysm.net/~japrime/lagenweb /shreve.htm *(Updated: 11/4/96) (Accessed 1/30/98)*

This public library has 23,000 volumes plus 22,000 rolls of microfilm. The materials in the genealogical and local history collection do not circulate. Up to ten photocopies are free to libraries that grant reciprocal services on interlibrary loan.

Maryland

Enoch Pratt Free Library
Maryland Depart., 400 Cathedral St., Baltimore, MD 21201-4484
Tel: 410-396-5468. Fax: 410-396-9537. Email: jKorman@mail.pratt.lib.md.us
URL: http://www.pratt.lib.md.us/pratt/depts/ md *(Updated 2/14/96) (Accessed 1/30/98)*
ILL: Yes

This is a major public library collection with 53,000 volumes in the genealogical collection. The library is open to the public and circulating materials circulate free to the public. Interlibrary loan is free to libraries that grant reciprocal loan privileges. Photocopies are 20¢ per page.

Michigan

Monroe County Library System
Ellis Reference and Information Center, 3700 South Custer, Monroe, MI 48161
Tel: 313-241-5277. Fax: 313-242-9037. Email: cjk@monroe.lib.mi.us
URL: http://www.monroe.lib.mi.us/ *(Updated: 1/15/98) (Accessed 1/3/98)*

The Monroe County Library System (MCLS) tries to help any genealogist who is conducting research in Michigan, northern Ohio, or Europe. Staff member Carl Katafiasz says, "We will do research for the genealogist, however, we will not do a complete genealogical profile. Since our service is free we see our role as an institution individuals can turn to for assistance when they run into a wall regarding a certain aspect of their family tree."

When asked to help with research they expect: (1) as much information as possible, (2) a copy of ancestral charts that can be written on, (3) a stamped self-addressed envelope, and (4) acknowledgment of remittance for copies at 25¢ per page.

Missouri

Springfield Greene County Library
Shepard Room–Main Library, P.O. Box 760, 397 E. Central, Springfield, MO 65802
Tel: 417-837-5050. Fax: 417-869-0320. Email: sheprm@mail.orion.org
URL: www.orion.org/library/sgcl/index.html *(Updated: 1/8/98) (Accessed 1/30/98)*

This library has an extensive local history and Missouri collection. The staff is happy to respond to specific inquiries that relate to their geographical area. Patrons must provide approximate dates, names, locations, and events. Some county histories may circulate. Photocopies are 25¢ per page plus a $3 service fee. The genealogy information on their Internet page (http://www.orion.org/library/sgcl /genea/geneanet.htm) has some nice links.

New Mexico

Albuquerque/Bernalillo County Library System
Special Collections Branch, 423 Central Ave. NE, Albuquerque, NM 87105-3517
Tel: 505-848-1376. Fax: 505-764-1574. Email: specialcollections@rgv.lib.nm.us
URL: http://www.cabq.gov./rgvls/specol.html *(Updated 8/12/97) (Accessed 1/30/98)*

This is a major public library with a significant genealogical collection consisting of 19,000+ books and 30,000 microforms. They own the microfilm for the entire United States from 1790–1870. Access is free and open to the public. Photocopies are free to libraries granting reciprocal borrowing privileges. Check with the library for mail-in requests.

North Carolina

Public Library of Charlotte and Mecklenburg County
Robinson-Spangler Carolina Rm., 310 North Tryon St., Charlotte, NC 28202
Tel: 704-336-2980. Email: ncr@plcmc.lib.nc.us
URL: http://www.plcmc.lib.nc.us/ *(Accessed 1/30/98)*
Online catalog: http://www.plcmc.lib.nc.us/online/catalog/default.htm (telnet)

This is a large public library with a 40,000 item genealogical and local history collection. Photocopies of specific citations will be made for $5 for up to twenty pages.

Pennsylvania

Erie County Library System
160 E. Front St., Erie, PA 16507
Tel: 814-451-6900. Fax: 814-541-6907. Email: ERIELIB@velocity.net
URL: www.ecls.lib.pa.us *(Accessed 1/30/98)*
ILL: Yes

This library will lend some genealogical materials on interlibrary loan except June through September. Photocopies through ILL are free. They charge individual patrons $1 per page if they call, send email, or mail their inquiries. Their online Obituary Listing indexes the obituaries that have appeared in the Erie newspapers from August of 1987 to the present.

Free Library of Philadelphia
1901 Vine St., Philadelphia, PA 19135
Tel: 215-686-5396. Fax: 215-686-5358. Email: stockw@library.phila.gov
URL: http://www.library.phila.gov/central/ssh/waltgen/geneal1.htm *(Updated 11/26/97) (Accessed 1/30/98)*
ILL: Yes

This is another major public library with significant research materials for genealogists. Interlibrary loan and photocopies are free to other libraries. Brief and to-the-point reference queries will be answered. Their Web site has many useful links for genealogists.

Rhode Island

Providence Public Library
225 Washington St., Providence, RI 02903
Tel: 401-455-8079. Fax: 401-455-8080
URL: http://www.clan.lib.ri.us/provide.htm *(Accessed 1/30/98)*
ILL: Yes, limited

Some genealogical materials may be borrowed through interlibrary loan. Check the online catalog for holdings.

Tennessee

Chattanooga-Hamilton County Bicentennial Library
Local History and Genealogy, 1001 Broad St., Chattanooga, TN 37402
Tel: 423-757-5317. No requests via email.
URL: http://www.lib.chattanooga.gov *(Updated: 8/30/97) (Accessed 1/30/98)*

This is a public library with a good genealogical collection and a staff that will do research for a fee. Requests require a $5 research fee which includes ten copies from printed materials or two copies from microfilm. Additional copies are 20¢ for books and 50¢ for microfilm. Mail-request research questions are limited to printed indexed resources.

Memphis/Shelby County Public Library
1850 Peabody Ave., Memphis, TN 38104
Tel: 901-725-8821. Fax: 901-725-8814. Email: hisref@memphis.lib.tn.us
URL: http://www.memphislibrary.lib.tn.us/infohub/htdrafts.htm *(Updated 12/8/97)*
(Accessed 1/30/98)

This public library has an extensive collection of historical and genealogical materials: 23,000 books and 12,000 reels of microfilms. A few duplicate copies of some books may circulate to library users in Shelby County. Inquiries received via regular mail should be brief and to the point. Enclose a self-addressed stamped envelope. Photocopies are 20¢ plus a $5 handling charge.

Public Library of Nashville and Davidson County
225 Polk Ave., Nashville, TN 37203
Tel: 901-862-5782. Email: nashville@waldo.nashv.lib.tn.us
URL: http://www.nashv.lib.tn.us *(Accessed 1/30/98)*

The Nashville Room has a collection of 30,000 books and microforms. If the library has extra copies of a book, they will lend it on ILL. For individuals, the library staff will search queries and photocopy materials for $15 per request. The fee includes ten photocopies. The fee for Tennessee residents who reside out of Davidson County is $5.

Texas

Dallas Public Library
1515 Young St., Dallas, TX 75201
Tel: 214-670-1433
URL: http://205.165.160.15/home.htm *(Updated 12/18/97) (Accessed 1/30/98)*
ILL: Yes

This public library has 70,000 volumes; 33,200 microfilms; 67,900 microfiche; and 1,240 micro cards. Interlibrary loan provides copies on request. Generally they do not charge. Because the online catalog does not list microforms, the best way to find out what the library has is to call and ask.

Houston Public Library
Clayton Lib. Center for Genealogical Research, 5300 Caroline St., Houston, TX 77004
Tel: 713-284-1999. Fax: 713-527-9447.
URL: http://www.hpl.lib.tx.us/hpl/clayton.html *(Updated: 12/1/97) (Accessed 1/30/98)*
Online catalog: http://www.hpl.lib.tx.us/hpl/hplb.html (telnet)

This public library has 60,000 books and 45,000 microprint dedicated to genealogical research. They will copy up to 50 pages. The charge is $1 per citation plus 25¢ per page. Suggested research technique: Identify a title in their online catalog, ask them to photocopy the section of the index that pertains to your research, then request copies of the pages with the best potential to contain the information needed.

Washington

Seattle Public Library
Humanities Department - Genealogy, 1000 4th Ave., Seattle, WA 98104-1193
Tel: 206-386-4629
URL: http://www.spl.lib.wa.us/ *(Updated 1/14/98) (Accessed 1/30/98)*
ILL: Yes

The Humanities Department has 22,000 volumes and 3,500 reels of microfilm. Through ILL they will lend some family and county histories. Photocopies are available through interlibrary loan.

Wyoming

Laramie County Public Library
Genealogy Depart., 2800 Central Ave., Cheyenne, WY 82001
Tel: 307-634-3561 ext. 144 or 132. Fax: 307 634-2082

The Laramie County Public Library has approximately 16,500 volumes in their genealogical and local history collection. Materials circulate free to Wyoming libraries through interlibrary loan. They charge other libraries for ILL. Up to ten pages are photocopied free to other libraries. The Cheyenne Genealogy Society provides up to 30 minutes of free research. Write to them in care of the library. A researcher will respond with any data found or suggestions for further research. Enclose a self-addressed stamped envelope with the request.

State Libraries & Archives

Alabama

Alabama Department of Archives and History
624 Washington Ave., P.O. Box 300100, Montgomery, AL 36130-0100
Tel: 334-242-4435. Fax: 334-240-3433. Email: ftaylor@dsmd.dsmd.state.al.us
URL: http://www.asc.edu/archives/agis.html *(Updated: 1/27/98) (Accessed 1/30/98)*

The Alabama Department of Archives and History is not primarily a genealogical library, but rather the state archives which includes materials of a genealogical nature (county records filmed by GSU, donated family history books and private manuscript collections). The staff will perform limited research using available indexes for individuals unable to visit the Archives for a fee of $15. Contact them for details.

California

California State Archives
1020 "O" St., Sacramento, CA 95814
Tel: 916-653-7715. Fax: 916-653-7363. Email: Archivesweb@ss.ca.gov
URL: http://www.ss.ca.gov/archives/archives_about.htm *(Accessed 1/30/98)*

This state archive has 60,000 cubic feet of archive material. The California State Archives collects, catalogs, preserves, and provides access to the historic records of state government and some local governments.

The California State Archives also houses the library collection of the Root Cellar of the Sacramento Genealogical Society. Check their Web site for fees.

Colorado

Colorado State Archives
1313 Sherman St., Rm. 1B-20, Denver, CO 80203
Tel: 303-866-2358. Fax: 303-866-2257
URL: http://webdig01.state.co.us/gov_dir/gss/archives/arcother.html *(Updated 6/7/96)*
(Accessed 1/30/98)

The Archives have statewide marriage and divorce indexes which span the years 1900–1939 and 1975–current. Consult specific counties for entries between 1940–1974. Some county indexes are held by the Archives, but most remain in the county of origin. The Colorado State Archives will respond to mail and phone requests, but their staff will suggest that if extensive research is required, that individuals visit their facility whenever possible.

Connecticut

Connecticut State Library, History and Genealogy Unit
231 Capitol Ave., Hartford, CT 06106-1537
Tel: 860-566-3690. Fax: 860-566-2133. Email: Rroberts@csl.ctstateu.edu
URL: http://www.cslnet.ctstateu.edu/handg.htm *(Accessed1/30/98)*
Online catalog: http://csulib.ctstateu.edu/search/d *(Accessed 1/30/98)*

This is an outstanding research facility for genealogists, whether they visit the library in person or request services from a distance. For a fee the History and Genealogy Unit's staff will spend up to one half hour responding to a written request. A single individual's name will be searched in statewide indexes, including: Barbour Collection of Town Vital Records, family and Bible records, Connecticut censuses, Connecticut newspaper marriage and death notice abstracts, the Hale Collection of Connecticut Cemetery Inscriptions, the Connecticut Church Record Abstracts, and the Connecticut Probate Estate Papers. They will not search resources that are not indexed, nor will they answer telephone requests. Write or check their Web site for details. Their online catalog works very well.

Delaware

Delaware Public Archives
Hall of Records, Dover, DE 19901
Tel: 302-739-5318
URL: http://del-aware.lib.de.us/archives/ *(Accessed 1/30/98)*

This is a state repository for vital records. Since 1913 vital records for Delaware have been collected and preserved here. Prior to 1913 the records were gathered in the counties and voluntarily sent to the state archive. They have birth, marriage, and death records available in a variety of formats.

The Delaware Public Archives also has copies of other archival records including all of the federal census population schedules 1790 to 1920, (except 1890).

Researchers can obtain information by writing to the Delaware Public Archives with pertinent information about the individual they are seeking. The staff will do minimal searching of available checklists and indexes. If the references are found, the staff will provide a price quote and reference. The minimum charge for copies is $5 for up to four pages. Additional charges apply for more photocopies plus $3 for shipping and handling.

Georgia

Georgia Department of Archives and History
330 Capitol Ave. SE, Atlanta, GA 30334
Tel: 404-656-2393. Fax: 404-657-8427
URL: http://www.sos.state.ga.us/archives *(Updated: 1/30/98)* *(Accessed 1/30/98)*

The Georgia Department of Archives and History collects, manages and preserves Georgia's historical records. It operates specialized libraries to make collections available to the public and government agencies. The Archives has extensive holdings of original records, microfilm copies of many pre-1900 county and federal records, published lists, abstracts, and other guides to these sources. Limited research can be performed by Archives staff for a non-refundable fee of $15 for Georgia residents and $25 for non-residents of Georgia.

Illinois

Illinois State Archive
Margaret Cross Norton Bldg., Springfield, IL 62756
Tel: 217-782-3492. Fax: 217-524-3930. Email: jdaly@ccgate.sos.state.il.us
URL: http://www.sos.state.il.us/depts/archives/arc_home.html (Slow to Load)
ILL: Yes

The Archive is the official depository for state and local government records which have long-term legal, administrative, historical, or research value. Of interest to genealogists the archives has court records, school records, military service records, birth records, and death records. This state archive is open to the public. Interlibrary loan is free to other libraries via the Illinois State Library. The Archives has a printed catalog that sells for $20.

Illinois State Historical Library
Old State Capitol, Springfield, IL 62701
Tel: 217-524-7216
URL: http://www.state.il.us/hpa/lib *(Updated 9/3/97) (Accessed 1/30/98)*
Online catalog: http://206.187.34.100 *(Accessed 1/30/98)*
ILL: Yes

This is an Illinois Historic Preservation Agency. They have 172,000 published books and 5,000 newspaper titles. Published books "may" be interlibrary loaned depending on age, condition, and the rarity of each title. Postage reimbursement is required for photocopies mailed to researchers. Up to ten photocopies are free to libraries that offer reciprocal borrowing privileges. Other libraries pay 25¢ per page.

The library staff will respond to requests for specific information that can be located in the collections. There is no charge for general historical research. Non-residents of Illinois are charged a $10 fee to research one family in one county. Illinois residents are not charged for research, but they are required to pay a minimal charge for photocopies.

Indiana

Indiana State Library
Genealogy Division, 140 N. Senate Ave., Indianapolis, IN 46204
Tel: 317-232-3689. Fax: 317-232-3728
URL: http://www.statelib.lib.in.us/ *(Accessed 1/30/98)*

This is a state agency that is open to the public. They have over 150,000 books, charts, pamphlets, and microforms. Genealogical materials do not circulate nor are they available on ILL. Some sources in other areas of the library, such as microfilmed newspapers, are available through interlibrary loan. Through the Web site, individuals may search the Index to Indiana Marriages through 1850 and the Indiana Cemetery Locator File. The Genealogy Division welcomes donations from individuals interested in sharing their research with others.

Iowa

State Historical Society of Iowa Library and Archives
600 East Locust, Capitol Complex, Des Moines, IA 50319
Tel: 515-281-6200. Fax: 515-282-0502
URL: http://www.uiowa.edu/~shsi/library/library.htm *(Accessed 1/30/98)*

This is both the state library and archives for Iowa, and it is open to the public. Researchers are welcome. Most of the collection of 75,000 books and 35,000 microfilms circulate to all libraries for a fee. The Society's reference staff will answer general history and genealogical research letters from Iowa residents only. The Society also has a list of professional researchers they will mail. Send a self-addressed stamped envelope.

Kansas

Kansas State Historical Society
6425 SW Sixth Ave., Topeka, KS 66615
Tel: 785-272-8681, ext. 117. Fax: 785-272-8682. TTY: 785-272-8683
URL: http://history.cc.ukans.edu/heritage/kshs/kshs1.html *(Accessed 1/30/98)*

The Kansas State Historical Society (KSHS) is the archives for Kansas. They have microfilmed every newspaper in the state. The staff will search card catalogs, indexes, and finding aids in response to requests for specific information. They will also search Kansas newspapers on microfilm for obituaries and other items when the patron can provide the following information: name of person, type of event, exact date of the event, exact location.

Staff will search for a maximum of two names per newspaper search request. Kansas residents and members of KSHS pay no fees. (Residence is determined by return address.) Photocopies cost 15¢ each with a minimum $2 charge. Copies requiring alternate copy methods will cost more. Out-of-state residents are charged

$10, payable at the time of the request. Responses will include up to five photocopies when information is available. Check out their award-winning Web site.

Kentucky

Kentucky Department for Libraries and Archives
300 Coffee Tree Rd., P.O. Box 537, Frankfort, KY 40602-0537
Tel: 502-564-8794 or 502-564-8300 ext. 347
URL: http://www.kdla.state.ky.us/ *(Updated 10/7/97) (Accessed 1/30/98)*

This public records repository contains almost 100,000 cubic feet of original materials and 45,000 rolls of microfilm. The Archives is a reference and research facility, and it does not lend its material. Federal census population schedules for Kentucky are available on interlibrary loan through public libraries and the Library Services Division of the Kentucky Department for Libraries and Archives. A list of persons willing to do research for a fee is available.

Louisiana

State Library of Louisiana
P.O. Box 31 (mailing), 701 North 4th St., Baton Rouge, LA 70821-0131
Tel: 504-342-4914. Fax: 504-342-3547. Email: ladept@pelican.state.lib.la.us
URL: http://smt.state.lib.la.us *(Updated 9/5/97) (Accessed 1/30/98)*
ILL: Yes

This state library has a collection of 5,000 genealogical books, and it is open to the public. Some of the material may circulate. They will make ILL duplicate copies of Louisiana genealogical materials, and copy up to five pages. In-state libraries are charged 10¢ per page. Copies for out-of-state libraries are 25¢. The Web site has links to state genealogical sites.

Maryland

Maryland State Archives
350 Rowe Blvd., Annapolis, MD 21401
Tel: 410-974-3914. Fax: 410-974-2525. Email: mdarchives@mdarchives.state.md.us
URL: http://www.mdarchives.state.md.us/ *(Accessed 1/30/98)*
ILL: Yes, to reciprocal libraries

The Maryland State Archives has a large collection of genealogical materials (175,000 cubic feet) that are open to the public. They loan microfilm on interlibrary loan to libraries that offer reciprocal borrowing services. Many of their documents are indexed on their search engine.

Massachusetts

State Library of Massachusetts
341 State House, Boston, MA 02133
Tel: 617-727-2590
URL: http://www.mlin.lib.ma.us/ *(Accessed 1/30/98)*

This state library has 800,000 volumes, plus material in other formats. The charges for photocopies depend on whether the researcher's library is a member of the network. The Massachusetts Library and Information Network is the researcher's guide to the library resources of Massachusetts. They can search public, academic, and special library catalogs throughout the state via the MLIN. This state library provides an access point to state, federal, and local government information.

Massachusetts State Archives
Office of Secretary of the Commonwealth, 220 Morrissey Blvd., Boston, MA 02125
Tel: 617-727-2816. Fax: 617-727-8730
URL: http://k12.oit.umass.edu/masag/1296o.html *(Accessed 1/30/98)*

This state archive has some vital records (1841–1900), immigration records and census schedules, select probate, naturalization and early court records. Items of interest in the Archives include: a series of 328 volumes of colonial papers, military records, charters, architectural plans and maps (some dating back to the earliest settlement period). Contact them for details on access.

Michigan

State Archives of Michigan
Michigan Historical Center, 717 W. Allegan St., Lansing, MI 48918-1837
Tel: 517-373-1408. Fax: 517-373-0851. Email: archives@sos.state.mi.us
URL: http://www.sos.state.mi.us/history/archive/archive.html *(Updated 1/6/98)*
(Accessed 1/30/98)

These archive holdings are particularly valuable for genealogical researchers. The State Archives of Michigan will accept limited email requests. Include the following in the body of your message: email address, subject of inquiry, your name, postal mailing address, and your telephone number.

They will conduct a maximum of ten minutes of research per request. Limit each request to one name, one record source, and date range (e.g., John Smith in Saginaw County naturalization records, 1900–1925). Charges: photocopies: 20¢ per page; microprints: 25¢ per page; certified copies: $1 per certification plus $1 per page. Payment should not be made in advance. Patrons will be sent an invoice for reproduction services. The *Michigan County Clerks Genealogy Directory*, is available on the Archives Web site and is a wonderful tool for genealogists, containing up-to-date information on each county.

New Hampshire

New Hampshire State Library
20 Park St., Concord, NH 03301
Tel: 271-6823. Fax: 603-271-2205. Email: ZMOORE@lilac.NHSL.LIB.NH.US
URL: http://www.state.nh.us/nhsl/ *(Updated 11/97)*
ILL: Yes

The New Hampshire State Library has 2,400 family histories and a name index to town records. Materials over one hundred years old do not circulate. They will ILL circulating copies of genealogical materials. Photocopies are free to other libraries, but individuals are charged.

New Jersey

New Jersey State Library
185 West State St., P.O. Box 520, Trenton, NJ 08625-0520
Tel: 609-292-6274. Fax: 609-984-7901. Email: Colesar@njsl.tesc.edu.
URL: http://www.state.nj.us/statelibrary/libgene.htm *(Updated 10/24/97)* *(Accessed 1/30/98)*

The genealogical research collection consists of guides, indexes, how-to-do-it books, periodicals, family genealogies and printed records, with a major emphasis on New Jersey and surrounding states. Included are the federal and state census records for New Jersey (1830–1920), and county and local histories.

Responses to written requests are limited to checking indexes, directories or bibliographies for information. For a fee the library will provide a limited number of photocopies. Original records such as birth, death and marriage records; deeds; and wills are housed in the New Jersey State Archives.

New York

New York State Archives
Cultural Education Center, Rm. 11D40, Albany, NY 12230
Tel: 518-474-8955. Fax: 518-473-9985. Email: refserv@unix6.nysed.gov
URL: http://www.sara.nysed.gov/services/research/inter.htm *(Updated 1/22/98)*
(Accessed 1/30/98)
ILL: Yes

Many of the records in the State Archives are available on microfilm. Researchers may borrow state records via interlibrary loan through their local public libraries or universities. The loan period is one month and the films may only be used in the borrowing library. The New York State Archives does not provide photocopy services via ILL, nor does it accept ILL orders via telefax or email.

North Carolina

North Carolina State Archives
Genealogical Research, 109 East Jones St., Raleigh, NC 27601-2807
Email: archives@ncsl.dcr.state.nc.us

URL: http://www.ah.dcr.state.nc.us/archives/arch/gen-res.htm *(Updated 1/22/98) (Accessed 1/30/98)*

Almost all of North Carolina's one hundred counties have forwarded their pre-1868 records, except deed and will books, to the Archives. At the Archives, each county's records are sorted into nine categories to facilitate research. Persons desiring to use the county records should be familiar with: *Guide to Research Materials in the North Carolina State Archives: County Records.* (North Carolina Archives, 1995. ISBN: 0-86526-277-2)

The Archives has a microfilm copy of every available decennial federal census from 1790–1920 (1890 was burned). The 1790 and 1820 censuses of North Carolina have been transcribed and published with an index.

Ohio

State Library of Ohio

Genealogy Section, 65 South Front St., Columbus, OH 43215-4163
Tel: 614-644-6966. Fax: 614-728-2789. Email: pkhouw@winslo.ohio.gov
URL: http://winslo.ohio.gov/
ILL: Yes

This is a state library with open access to the public. They will only lend materials for which they have a duplicate copy in the collection. The basic research fee for all general requests (prepaid) is $3 (plus 18¢ tax for Ohio residents). This search fee is for one question or name, and includes up to ten photocopied pages. Up to ten photocopies are free to other libraries.

The collection is accessible through the Online Computer Library Center (OCLC). For those unable to research in person, the correspondence policy allows staff to check one family name in one Ohio county. For indexed information, printed resources will be sent for $1 for five pages or less. Additional copies are 20¢ each.

Oregon

Oregon State Archives

800 Summer St. NE, Salem, OR 97310
Tel: 503-373-0701. Fax: 503-373-0953. Email: reference.archives@state.or.us
URL: http://arcweb.sos.state.or.us/ *(Accessed 1/30/98)*

The reference staff welcomes email reference requests. Limit requests to two named individuals and one record source at a time. Include your postal mailing address in the message. If photocopies are requested, you will be notified of any charges in the accompanying return letter. Contact them for specific charges.

The Oregon State Archives has a search engine at their Web site called the Genealogical Information Locator that will help locate information of genealogical value.

Pennsylvania

State Library of Pennsylvania

P.O. Box 1601, Forum Bldg., Harrisburg, PA 17105-1601
Tel: 717-787-4440. Fax: 717-783-2070. Email: Ali@stlib.state.pa.us
URL: http://www.cas.psu.edu/docs/pde/LIBCOLL.HTML *(Accessed 1/30/98)*
Online catalog: http://accesspa.brodart.com.
ILL: Yes, to Pennsylvania libraries

This collection contains important Pennsylvania genealogies and local histories, including several hundred unpublished compilations of church and cemetery records. Approximately 13,500 titles are in microform, including federal census records for Pennsylvania from 1790–1920. Among the unique indexes for genealogical research is a surname and place-name card file. Genealogy and local history materials must be used on-site and cannot be borrowed.

South Carolina

South Carolina Department of Archives and History

P.O. Box 11669, Columbia, SC 29211
Tel: 803-734-8577. Fax: 803-734-8820. Email: tuttle@history.scdah.sc.edu
URL: http://www.scdah.sc.edu/homepage.htm

This state archive has a checklist of useful records, indexes, guides, and publications for genealogical research. South Carolina required marriage licenses beginning in

1911 and birth and death certificates beginning in 1915. The Reference Services Branch answers all genealogical queries. The staff will answer questions about the records and provide specific information if the amount of research time is reasonable. Staff will also check specified indexes for a specific name and fill a photocopy order for records in which the name appears. For mail or Internet requests the staff will check pertinent sources if provided with the name of an individual, county and approximate dates of residence in South Carolina. Limit index checks to one name per request. Indexes searched include land records, probate records, and military records.

If any information is found about the individual, the staff will provide price quotes for copies of up to ten records per request. Indexes and records will be quoted as they appear. They cannot verify identities, check the contents of records, or attempt to determine parentage. Do not send money until you receive an order form listing the cost of copies of materials located by the staff. When you return the form with payment, they will process your order.

South Dakota

South Dakota State Archives

900 Governor's Dr., Pierre, SD 57501
Tel: 605-773-3804. Fax: 605-773-6041. Email: archref@chc.state.sd.us
URL: http://www.state.sd.us/state/executive/deca/cultural/archives.htm *(Updated 9/19/97)* *(Accessed 1/30/98)*

The South Dakota State Archives is a repository for public documents. They have a collection of approximately 90,000 volumes. The stacks are closed and materials do not circulate. They will loan microfilm for a fee. Photocopies are 25¢ per page. Extensive reference requests require a prepaid research fee. Their Web site has search engines that help with genealogical research.

Tennessee

Tennessee State Library and Archives

403 7th Ave. North, Nashville, TN 37243-0312
Tel: 615 741-2764. Fax: 615-532-2472. Email: reference@mail.state.tn.us
URL: http://www.state.tn.us/sos/statelib/ *(Accessed 1/30/98)*
ILL: Yes

This is a state library and archive with a collection of 775,00 volumes and four million manuscripts. The facility is open to the public. They will only lend duplicate copies on interlibrary loan. Indexes to pre-1860 wills, marriages and deeds on microfilm are also available on ILL. A research service is available by mail: $5 to search for a specific document when a name, county of residence, type of record and approximate year are provided. Photocopies are $3.

Texas

Texas State Library and Archives Commission

P.O. Box 12927 (mailing), 1201 Brazos St., Austin, TX 78711
Tel: 512-463-5463. Fax: 512-463-5436. Email: geninfo@tsl.state.tx.us
URL: www.tsl.state.tx.us/lobby *(Updated 8/12/97)* *(Accessed 1/30/98)*

This state library and archive has 20,000 volumes and 2,800 reels of microfilm or microfiche. The facility is free and open to the public. They lend genealogical materials for which they have duplicates in the collection. Up to ten photocopies are free to other libraries. The staff will respond to questions by mail. In the request include: the full name of the individual, the specific record being sought, approximate date, and city and county where the record was created or the person resided. They will send a bill for the research.

Utah

Utah State Archives

P.O. Box 141021 (mailing), Salt Lake City, UT 84114-1021
Tel: 801-538-3013. Fax: 801-538-3354. Email: research@state.ut.us
URL: http://www.archives.state.ut.us/ *(Accessed 1/30/98)*

The Utah State Archives' Research Center is located in Salt Lake City behind the State Capitol and State Office Building. The Archives consist of microfilmed state and local government records of permanent historical value. Public records that have been microfilmed can also be purchased at cost or borrowed for the cost of delivery and mailed to your home or institution.

Some of the records genealogists find useful are: military records and discharges, and court records (divorces, criminal and civil files, probate records, naturalizations, and birth, marriage, and death records, 1898–1905.) Other records are available in individual counties.

Vermont

Vermont Department of Libraries

109 State St., Montpelier, VT 05609-0601
Tel: 802-828-3261. Fax: 802-828-2199. Email: RLS@dol.state.vt.us
URL: http://dol.state.vt.us/ *(Accessed 1/30/98)*
ILL: Yes

The Department will loan materials and make up to ten photocopies free of charge for other libraries. The collection includes the Vermont census on microfilm and Vermont newspapers on microfilm. Census films circulate through ILL if a second copy is on hand for local research. Newspaper microfilm circulate through ILL with a four reel maximum.

Virginia

The Library of Virginia

800 East Broad St., Richmond, VA 23219-1905
Tel: 804-692-3777 (Library Reference)
Tel: 804-692-3888 (Archives Reference). Fax: 804-692-3556.
URL: http://leo.vsla.edu *(Accessed 1/30/98)*
ILL: Virginia libraries only

This state library is open to the public. It has 1.5 million volumes, 80 million manuscripts, and 66,000 maps. ILL is free to other Virginia libraries. No ILL is available for out-of-state libraries. Up to ten photocopies are free to other libraries. Write for free pamphlet: "Genealogical Research at The Library of Virginia." Research inquiries from outside Virginia are assessed a service fee of $10.

The library's home page features indexes and links to digital images of several collections of original records, photographs, and maps. The digital collections of family bible records and land office patents and grants are especially popular.

West Virginia

West Virginia State Archives

Archives & History Lib., Cultural Center, 1900 Kanawha Blvd. E, Charleston, WV 25305-0300
URL: http://www.wvlc.wvnet.edu/history/wvsamenu.html *(Updated 1/15/98) (Accessed 1/30/98)*

The Archives will not answer email research requests. All research requests must be submitted in writing. Requests from outside West Virginia must be accompanied by a $10 research fee (checks made payable to the West Virginia Division of Culture and History). Check their Web site for details on services and costs.

The *West Virginia History Database* has many links that genealogists will appreciate, including a surname exchange database.

Wisconsin

State Historical Society of Wisconsin

816 State St., Madison, WI 53706
Tel: 608-264-6460. Fax: 608-264-6486. Email: archives.reference@ccmail.adp.wisc.edu
URL: http://www.wisc.edu/shs-archives/ *(Updated 11/21/97) (Accessed 1/30/98)*

Staff members cannot undertake extensive research, but they will respond to reasonable requests for information about or from the Archives holdings. Mail, email and telephone requests are generally answered in the order they are received and may take two to four weeks for a response, depending on the backlog. Check their Web site for an email request form.

Wyoming

Wyoming State Archives

Barrett Building, 2301 Central Ave., Cheyenne, WY 82001
Tel: 307-777-7826. Fax: 307-777-7044. Email: wyarchive@missc.state.wy.us

URL: http://commerce.state.wy.us/CR/Archives/ *(Accessed 1/30/98)*

This is another state archive that is open to the public. They collect and manage public records for Wyoming state departments and local governments that have legal and historical value. These records document the activities of government in Wyoming and the history of the state. The records are available for research. Copies are 50¢ per page to everyone. Check the Web site to see which state and county records are available.

Historical Societies

California

Immigrant Genealogical Society Library
1310-B W. Magnolia Blvd., P.O. Box 7369, Burbank, CA 91510-7369
Tel: 818-848-3122. Fax: None. Email: NEPSUND@aol.com (Research Director)
URL: http://feefhs.org/igs/frg-igs.html *(Accessed 1/30/98)*

This is a special library focussed on German research. They have many sources not available in Salt Lake City. Access is free and open to members; others pay a daily fee of $2. They do research by mail for anyone. Contact them for a fee schedule.

Colorado

Colorado Historical Society
Stephen H. Hart Library, 1300 Broadway, Denver, CO 80203
Tel: 303-866-2305. Fax: 303-866-5739. Email: chssysop@usa.net
URL: http://www.gtownloop.com/chs.html *(Accessed 1/30/98)*

This is a publicly funded library that has 45,000 books; 5,000 maps; 1,750 serial titles; 2,500 newspaper titles; 2,000 manuscript collections and 50,000 photos. This is one of the West's most comprehensive history libraries and it is open to the public. They provide discounted assistance to members, and they will copy materials that are not harmed by the photocopy process.

Florida

South Suburban Genealogical and Historical Society Library
320 E. 161st Pl., P.O. Box 96 (mailing), South Holland, FL 60473
Tel: 708-333-9474
URL: http://www.rootsweb.com/~ssghs/ssghs.htm *(Updated 11/5/97) (Accessed 1/30/98)*

This historical society library has 7,000 volumes, microforms, maps, and CD-ROMs. Copies are 10¢ per page plus the copyist's time. They have a printed catalog that sells for $4. Researchers can search the collection for $10 per hour. Send a self-addressed stamped envelope with query. Check out their attractive Web site for more information.

Georgia

Georgia Historical Society
501 Whitaker St., Savannah, GA 31499
Tel: 912-651-2128. Fax: 912-651-2831. Email: gahist@ix.netcom.com
URL: http://www.savannah-online.com/ghs/ *(Accessed 1/30/98)*

This privately funded society library is open to the public. They have 17,000 volumes, microforms, archives, and manuscripts (4,000 cubic feet). The collection is cataloged on OCLC. Photocopies are 15¢ to members and 30¢ to non-members. Check their Web site for more information.

Idaho

Idaho Historical Society Genealogy Library
450 N. 4th St., Boise, ID 83702
Tel: 208-334-3357. Fax: 208-334-3198
ILL: Yes

This is a special library open to the public with 20,000 volumes including all of the federal census population schedules, 1790–1920. They lend census and newspaper microfilm for the cost of shipping. Photocopies are 25¢ per page.

Indiana

William Henry Smith Memorial Library of the Indiana Historical Society

315 West Ohio St., Indianapolis, IN 46202-3299
Tel: 317-232-1879. Fax: 317-233-3109. Email: emundell@statelib.lib.in.us
URL: http://www.ihs1830.org/ *(Accessed 1/30/98)*
ILL: Yes

Although the Smith Library is not a genealogical library per se, many of its collections and other materials can be used to conduct genealogical research. Staff will spend up to 30 minutes researching and responding to a specific question sent via mail, fax, email, etc. They will also recommend researchers whom interested patrons can contract to do genealogical research (performance, however, is not guaranteed by IHS).

Kansas

Heart of America Genealogical Society and Library Inc.

c/o Kansas City Public Library, 311 E. 12th St., Kansas City, MO 64106-2412
Tel: 816-221-2685 ext. 71

This is a society library, within the Kansas City Public Library, that is supported with membership dues, but is open to the public. The collection emphasizes family books, county histories, periodicals, and member lineage charts. Materials circulate locally only. Research and photocopying are done by volunteers. Limited research may be requested by mail for which a donation is expected along with a self-addressed stamped envelope.

Kentucky

Kentucky Historical Society

300 Broadway, Box 1792, Frankfort, KY 40602
Tel: 502-564-3016. Fax: 502-564-4701

This is a state historical society with 80,000 volumes. Their facilities and collections are open to the public at no charge. Up to ten photocopies are free to other libraries. Copies by mail to individuals are 50¢ each.

Sons of the American Revolution Library

1000 South 4th St., Louisville, KY 40203
Tel: 502-589-1776. Fax: 502-589-1671. Email: LIBRARY@SAR.ORG

This special library has 50,000 volumes including film, fiche and CD-ROMs. It is supported through memberships and user fees. They will copy and mail specifically requested pages for a fee.

Massachusetts

American Antiquarian Society

185 Salisbury St., Worcester, MA 01609
Tel: 508-775-5221. Fax: 508-753-3311. Email: library@mwa.org
URL: gopher://mark.mwa.org *(Accessed 1/30/98)*

This is a privately funded special library that is open to the public. They have 17,500 genealogies and 60,000 local histories. With holdings numbering close to three million books, pamphlets, broadsides, manuscripts, prints, maps and newspapers, this library preserves the largest single collection of printed source material relating to the history, literature, and culture of the first 250 years of what is now the United States. Depending on the condition of the item, photocopies may be made for 20¢ per page plus a $5 handling fee and postage.

Minnesota

Minnesota Historical Society

Research Center, 345 Kellogg Blvd. West, St. Paul, MN 55102-1906
Tel: 612-296-6143. Fax: 612-296-7436. Email: reference@mnhs.org
URL: http://www.mnhs.org/ebranch/mhs/index.html *(Accessed 1/30/98)*

This is a joint public and privately funded research center with 500,000 volumes, and it is open to the public. They do not lend books, but they do lend most of their genealogical microfilms. Their photocopy charge is 20¢ per page plus $2 for shipping

ILL materials. All reference requests should be addressed to the Reference Associate. They have an exceptional Web site.

Nebraska

Nebraska State Historical Society
P.O. Box 82554, 1500 "R" St., Lincoln, NE 68503
Tel: 402-471-4751. Fax: 402-471-3600. Email: lanshs@inetnebr.com

The Society lends microfilm copies of Nebraska newspapers, manuscripts, public records, library materials, and National Archives microfilm for which they have master copies. The charge is $5 per roll and the limit is two rolls per patron. Libraries in the U.S. and Canada may request microfilm using standard interlibrary loan forms. Borrowed films must be used in the library that borrowed them. Prepayment is required. Contact them for complete summaries of their holdings.

American Historical Society of Germans from Russia Archives
631 D St., Lincoln, NE 68502
Tel: 402-474-3363. Fax: 402-474-7229. Email: ahsgr@aol.com
URL: http://www.ahsgr.org/ *(Accessed 1/30/98)*
ILL: Yes through OCLC

This is a special archive with approximately 10,000 titles specializing in the heritage of Germans from Russia. The Archive is open to the public at no charge. They participate in interlibrary loan through OCLC. Photocopies are $1 per page. Their Web site is a gold mine of information and research links.

Ohio

Ohio Historical Society
1982 Velma Ave., Columbus, OH 43211-2497
Tel: 614-297-2510. Fax: 614-279-2546. Email: ohref@winslo.state.oh.us
URL: http://www.ohiohistory.org *(Accessed 1/30/98)*

This is a publicly supported historical society. Interlibrary loan is available for materials for which the society holds the original or the negative, including newspapers, the Ohio county history surname index, county histories, and manuscripts. ILL orders must be submitted through a library on an ALA ILL form and payment of $3 per film must be enclosed. Check out their Web site. It is very attractive and has a lot to offer.

Research staff will answer specific reference requests by mail. Research time is limited to twenty minutes per request. No newspaper or obituary searches are conducted. The fee is $3 plus tax, which includes up to ten photocopies. Additional copies are 25¢.

Oklahoma

Oklahoma Historical Society
Research Library and Archives, 2100 North Lincoln Blvd., Oklahoma City, OK 73105
Tel: 405-522-5225. Fax: 405-521-2492
URL: http://www.coax.net/people/LWF/ohsres.htm *(Accessed 2/4/98)*

This historical society library has 66,000 volumes and is open to the public. Researchers need not be historians or scholars to find the facilities useful. Knowledgeable staff members are available in all areas to assist researchers in the use of microfilm, card catalogs, census and enrollment books, and other finding aids. Research fees for out-of-state mail requests are $15 per hour. Copies are 20¢each. Faxed copies are $1. Any charges will be invoiced; see their Web site for a fee schedule.

Oregon

Oregon Genealogical Society
P.O. Box 10306 (mailing), 223 N. "A" St., Ste. F, Springfield, OR 97477
Tel: 541-746-7924
URL: http://www.rootsweb.com/~genepool/ogsinfo.htm *(Accessed 1/30/98)*

This is a society library that is open to the public for a fee or by membership. They have 6,000 titles and 3,000 periodicals. Some materials circulate to members free. They will do research for $7.50 per hour plus expenses. They charge 10¢ per page for photocopies.

Pennsylvania

Historical Society of Pennsylvania

1300 Locust St., Philadelphia, PA 19107-5699
Tel: 215-732-6200. Fax: 215-732-2680. Email: hsppr@aol.com
URL: http://www.libertynet.org/~pahist *(Updated 1/25/98) (Accessed 1/30/98)*
Research by mail.

This is a special library that is privately funded and open to members; non-members pay a fee. They have 10,000 published genealogies and 30,000 in manuscript form. The research-by-mail service of the Historical Society of Pennsylvania is the largest independent center for research in Pennsylvania and the largest genealogy center in the mid-Atlantic region. Rates are $25 to $50 per hour depending on membership and priority.

Texas

Daughters of the Republic of Texas Library

P.O. Box 1401, San Antonio, TX 78295-1401
Tel: 210-225-1071. Fax: 210-212-8514. Email: drtl@salsa.net
URL: http://www.drtl.org *(Updated: 12/17/97) (Accessed 1/30/98)*

The Daughters of the Republic of Texas Library is part of the Alamo historical complex in San Antonio. The non-circulating collection pertains to the history of Texas, San Antonio, and the Alamo.

Written and telephone requests for information are welcome. Make requests for information as specific as possible. All written and telephone requests require prepayment of $7 to cover the cost of photocopying, postage and handling, and limited research time. Checks should be made payable to the DRT Library Committee. If the request requires lengthy research the library will supply a list of professional researchers. Photocopies are 20–30¢ per page depending on the size.

Virginia

Albemarle County Historical Society Library

200 2nd St. NE, The McIntire Building, Charlottesville, VA 22902
Tel: 804-296-7294. Fax: 804-296-4576
URL: http://monticello.avenue.gen.va.us/Community/Agencies/ACHS/ *(Updated 8/97)
(Accessed 1/30/98)*

This library is operated jointly with the local public library. If the condition of the material permits, photocopies may be made of specific titles at 15¢ per page for libraries that offer reciprocal services.

Virginia Historical Society

P.O. Box 7311, 428 N. Blvd., Richmond, VA 23221
Tel: 804-342-9677. Fax: 804-355-2399
URL: http://www.vahistorical.org *(Updated 1/22/98) (Accessed 1/30/98)*

This is a special library open to the public, but non-members pay $4. They have an extensive collection of one hundred thousand volumes and seven million manuscripts. For $10 and 25¢ a page they will research a question and send copies.

Wisconsin

Racine Heritage Museum and Archive

701 S. Main St., Racine, WI 53403-1211
Tel: 414-636-3626. Fax: 414-636-3940

If your research takes you to Racine County, Wisconsin, you will find many helpful resources at the Racine Heritage Museum and Archive. This is a privately funded archive that is open to the public on specified days and times. They have good cemetery records, a fine card file with cross references, and excellent Civil War soldier records, all limited to Racine County. Researchers may request information by mail. Send at least $10 and a self-addressed stamped envelope with your request. Volunteers will respond to requests in the order they are received.

Academic Libraries

Texas

Angelo State University

West Texas Collection, Porter Henderson Lib., P.O. Box 11013, San Angelo, TX 76909
Tel: 915-942-2164. Fax: 915-942-2190. Email: Susanne.Campbell@angelo.edu
URL: http://www.angelo.edu/~library/ *(Updated 1/21/98) (Accessed 1/30/98)*
ILL: Second copies only

This is an academic library that is open to the public. They have 7,800 volumes, 2,300 reels of microfilm, plus archives. Photocopy service is free to other libraries. Their catalog is accessible through their Web site.

East Texas Research Center

P.O. Box 13055, SFA Sta., Stephen F. Austin State Univ., Nacogdoches, TX 75962-3055
Tel: 409-468-4100. Fax: 409-468-7610. Email: AskETRC@sfalib.sfasu.edu
URL: http://libweb.sfasu.edu/etrc/etrchome.htm *(Updated 1/98) (Accessed 1/30/98)*
Online catalog: http://libweb.sfasu.edu/etrc/etrcbro.htm *(Updated 1/98) (Accessed 1/30/98)*
ILL: Yes

This library/archive has 14,566 linear feet of books and manuscripts. State-owned microfilm may circulate to other libraries on ILL. All other materials do not circulate. Researchers are asked to send 10¢ per page for photocopies plus postage.

Harold B. Simpson Hill College History Complex

P.O. Box 619, Hillsboro, TX 76645
Tel: 254-582-2555 ext. 242
URL: http://hillcollege.hill-college.cc.tx.us/ *(Updated 1/98) (Accessed 1/30/98)*

The Confederate Research Center and Museum at this college has over 5,000 books, brochures, and pamphlets on the Civil War with emphasis on Confederate military history. For a $15 research fee they will search their indexes and send copies of the information they find. Request their form with a SASE before submitting a research inquiry.

Utah

Brigham Young University

Utah Valley Reg. Family History Center, Harold Lee Library, 3080 HBLL, Provo, UT 84602
Tel: 801-378-2905. Fax: 801-378-6708.
URL: http://www.lib.byu.edu/~uvrfhc/ *(Accessed 1/30/98)*

Housed on the fourth floor of the Harold B. Lee Library, the Utah Valley Regional Family History Center is one of the major Centers in the Family History Library network. It has thousands of rolls of microfilm on indefinite loan from the Family History Library. It also has a large collection of books and periodicals containing significant genealogical information. There is also a respectable collection CD-ROMs for genealogical research. Volunteer consultants are available to assist with genealogical questions and research. County histories are available in the library's book and microfiche collections. See the BYU Library Catalog for information on availability.

West Virginia

West Virginia and Regional History Collection

West Virginia Univ. Libraries, Colson Hall, P.O. Box 6464, Morgantown, WV 26506-6464
Tel: 304-293-3536. Fax: 304-293-3981
URL: www.wvu.edu:80/~library/collect.htm *(Updated 1/97) (Accessed 1/30/98)*

This collection has 40,000 books and 4.5 million manuscripts. It is open to the public. The minimum photocopy charge is $10 which includes 50 pages. Copies are 15¢ per page beyond the first 50.

Wyoming

University of Wyoming

American Heritage Center, P.O. Box 3824, Laramie, WY 82071-3924
Tel: 307-766-4114. Fax: 307-766-5511. Email: AHCREF@uwyo.edu
URL: http://www.uwyo.edu/lib/home.htm *(Updated 1/27/98) (Accessed 1/30/98)*
Online catalog: telnet://csn.carl.org

The American Heritage Center is a research facility at the University of Wyoming. It houses a large collection (75,000 cubic feet). The library is open to the public, but the materials do not circulate. The reference staff will assist researchers who cannot come to the center with research requests. Research requests may be submitted via telephone, letter, or email. There is no charge for this service, however, if photocopies of materials are sent to the researcher, charges will apply.

Commercial Libraries

Pennsylvania

Hoenstine Rental Library
414 Montgomery St., Hollidaysburg, PA 16648
Tel: 814-695-0632. Fax: 814-696-7310
URL: http://ourworld.compuserve.com/homepages/LLewis/hoenstin.htm *(Accessed 1/30/98)*

The Hoenstine Rental Library is a private library that charges a fee for access. They rent materials to individuals through the mail. Requests should include a deposit that approximates the cost of the book. When the material is returned, 75 percent of the deposit is refunded. The balance is rent for the 30-day rental period. Access to the collection is through their printed catalog which sells for $75. Contact them for more details.

Utah

Everton's Genealogical Library
3223 S. Main, Nibley, UT 84332
Tel: 1-800-443-6325. Fax: 801-752-0425. Order@everton.com.
URL: http://www.everton.com *(Accessed 1/30/98)*

This is a private library supported by Everton Publishers that is free and open to the public. Members can access many resources online, including their Root Cellar. Photocopies are 10¢ per page.

Special Libraries & Archives

Illinois

Newberry Library
60 W. Walton, Chicago, IL 60610
Tel: 312-943-9090. Fax: 312-255-3513
URL: http://www.newberry.org *(Accessed 6/30/98)*

This privately funded library has approximately 200,000 titles of local and family history, making it one of the largest collections of its kind in the world. Materials do not circulate, but the research resources of the library are tremendous. Published bibliographies and other pathfinders on their Web site will help researchers locate materials in the collection.

Indiana

Mennonite Historical Library
Goshen College, Goshen, IN 46526-4794
Tel: 219-535-7418. Fax: 219-535-7438. Email: joeas@goshen.edu
URL: http://www.goshen.edu/library/ *(Updated 1/15/98) (Accessed 1/30/98)*

This organization holds a rich collection of materials relating to three centuries of Mennonite and eastern Pennsylvania history and culture. Photocopy service is 15¢ per page plus postage, with a minimum fee of $3. Admission is $3 a day.

Louisiana

Diocese of Baton Rouge
Department of Archives, P.O. Box 2028, Baton Rouge, LA 70821-2028
Tel: 504-387-0561 ext. 320

The Department of Archives is the repository of the sacrament records of the Catholic churches within the Diocese of Baton Rouge. Baptismal, marriage and burial information from the church records is available to researchers at a nominal fee. Dates of their records range from 1707 to 1888. Archival holdings generally do not include records after 1900. These records are still housed at the individual churches.

Certificates, where no research is required, may be obtained for $3 per certificate plus 50¢ for mailing expenses. Photocopies of the original records from microfilm are available. The charge for each copy is $7.50. One photocopy plus a typed certificate is $10. If the original is too poor to reproduce, your money will be returned. Research on an individual basis is $6 for the first hour, each additional hour costs $5. Research, such as ancestor charts or family groups sheets, may be done by mail or in person. No request can be submitted by telephone. In-person searches require an appointment.

Ohio

Jacob Rader Marcus Center of the American Jewish Archives

3101 Clifton Ave., Cincinnati, OH 45220-2488
Tel: 513-221-1875. Fax: 513-221-7812. Email: AJA@fuse.net
URL: http://home.fuse.net/aja/Archive.htm *(Accessed 1/30/98)*

This privately funded special archive will lend microfilm on interlibrary loan. Check their online catalog to find out what is in the collection. Up to ten photocopied pages are free to other libraries. The American Jewish Archives is open to all users.

Pennsylvania

Archives and Records Center—Synod Hall

125 N. Craig St., Pittsburgh, PA 15213
Tel: (412) 621-6217. Fax: (412) 621-6237. Email: archives@diopitt.org
URL: http://www.diopitt.org/arcinfo.htm *(Accessed 1/30/98)*

The Archives maintains five types of sacramental records: baptismal, first communion, confirmation, marriage and death registers. Only sacramental records older than one hundred years are open for genealogical research. The actual search can only be done by Archives staff due to privacy considerations. All research requests must be in writing and must include a $15 deposit. Research request forms are available from the Archives.

Note: Diocese archives are potentially good sources of genealogical information. Use one of the search engines on the Internet. Search: +Diocese +Archive +(city)

Using this List

If a patron from your library needs research in another state, this list will give you a starting point for the research. Here are some ideas you can use to help your customers:

- Call the staff in that institution and ask about their services.

- Visit their Web site, if they have one, to learn more about their genealogical collection.

- Check their online catalog, if they have one, to see what they have.

- Send a request to that library for your patron, or

- Give your patron the information so they can make a request.

- Compare and contrast the services provided by these libraries, using the ones you like as models for your own program.

Chapter 7

Using Computers–Genealogy Software

In 1996, I put part of my genealogy on the Internet along with my email address. Several times a week I now get queries from people who think we might be related. Recently I received a query about my Boggess line from West Virginia. I have lots of information on this line. When Diana Jones told me where she was born and who her ancestors were, I knew we were distant cousins. As it turned out, we are related on two lines. She was very excited to be able to extend her family tree. I was glad to find another cousin who had some family information I didn't have.

Computers and genealogy are meant for each other. Genealogists need to organize and store their research. Doing what they do so well, computers stockpile and retrieve that data, display it, and print it in lots of useful ways. Over the years, at the same time that personal computers were becoming increasingly powerful and reliable, their cost was steadily falling.

And now, the power of the Internet makes it easy for genealogists to share the data they have collected and stored on their personal computers with the simple addition of a modem and telephone line. This sharing of information has created an explosion in genealogy activity. Family historians can get on the Internet to look for the names of the people they are researching. When they find one they think might be a match, they can send an email message to the person who mounted the page. Looking at the tools that integrate all of these tasks, I have focused this chapter on the genealogy software currently available to help organize, record, retrieve, copy, and share genealogical research.

CD-ROM Technology

Although its popularity seems to be waning, I would would like to say a few words about CD-ROM tools for genealogists. I don't believe CD-ROM technology will soon disappear because of its excellent data storage capability. In the earlier days of CD-ROM technology, hard drive capacity made them very attractive. In fact, many products that required extremely large amounts of storage, like encyclopedias or very large databases like the *International Genealogical Index*, were ideally suited for CD-ROM production. Today, with the cost of CDs decreasing, they are well within the budget of many individuals.

Some genealogical publishing companies are commercially successful because they have placed their genealogical databases on CD-ROM. Family Tree Maker, a division of Broderbund, has several databases on CD entitled *Family Archives*. They are reasonably priced for individuals or libraries. When technologists get the quirks of Optical Character Recognition worked out, we will see thousands of volumes of printed historical records on CD. This will permit genealogists to search the text for names. An index won't be necessary, because the search engine will take us right to the text.

Focusing on Software

Creating a standard

In the early history of personal computers some genealogists and computer programmers began exploring ways to enter genealogical data, organize it, display it and print it out in traditional genealogical formats. As often is the case in the infancy of technology development, there was no standard and every developer had his or her own way of handling data. At this time, the Personal Ancestral File (PAF) was developed by the Family History Library, and soon became a leader in the field. Leland

Mietzler, Executive Editor of *Heritage Quest Magazine*, recalls developers of various genealogy software products coming together in Salt Lake City in 1987. Working for The Church of Jesus Christ of Latter-day Saints, the developers of the Personal Ancestral File proposed development of a standard protocol for the exchange of genealogical data and GEDCOM (Genealogical Data Communication) was born. As more genealogy software developers started using it, GEDCOM became a standard way of transferring genealogical data between different genealogy programs. It remains the standard in the industry today. Any producer of a genealogy software product that wants to compete in the market must include GEDCOM compatibility, and it was considered essential for any software mentioned in this chapter.

Selecting genealogy software

Buying a software package to manage your genealogy is not quite like buying a new car, but still, if you make an ill-advised choice, hours of data entry may be wasted on a program you decide to drop. If the replacement program isn't compatible with the old one, you may not be able to transfer the data. That is why GEDCOM is absolutely essential.

There isn't enough room in this chapter to list all of the features every program offers. The best a prospective buyer can do is to learn as much as possible about the major programs, and then make an informed decision. Some vendors offer a trial disk containing the software to prospective buyers for a $5 charge that can be credited towards the purchase. You can try them out and then decide. A librarian might consider buying and loading several software programs to let patrons try them out on one of the library's public access computers.

Innovations and new releases are coming out all the time, so the best place obtain current information on genealogy software is through the Internet. Check the Web sites I have listed starting on p. 93. Using a search engine, you may want to check on a specific software by typing in the name of the software, "+evaluation," "+comments," "+users." Keeping up with genealogy software features and owners is a difficult task—even on the Internet. Where available I have provided a current URL for each of the software programs listed.

Software Selection Checklist

✔ *Adding individuals:* Is it easy to enter new individuals, parents, children or spouses from a single screen or to quickly toggle from screen to screen? After the initial entry that transfers your genealogy from paper copy to the computer, data input is rarely linear. You need the flexibility of moving from one individual or family to another easily.

✔ *Backup:* Does the program offer easy-to-use backup procedures, or reminders to backup the data? You should backup your data every time you add something to the database. If the process is cumbersome, or if you are not reminded to do it, you might skip it.

✔ *Biography:* Does the software offer expanded capacity for biographical information? If you are creating a family record as well as collecting genealogical data, you will want to have plenty of room for biographical and anecdotal material.

✔ *Browse:* Can you browse up and down the pedigree chart or the entire database? Many times you may find a name or other piece of data that may apply to your research. The name may not be exact, but other pieces of information fit. You will want to browse the list for other bits of information that will help you make the connection, such as parents, marriage date, spouse, birth date, death date, etc.

✔ *Calculator:* Does the program include a dates, ages, life expectancy calculator? This is a useful little tool. Not essential, but nice to have.

✔ *Capacity:* How many names, facts, events, etc. will the database hold? This is an important issue, but most of the programs seem to have more capacity than most genealogists will ever want.

✔ *Compatibility:* Does the program have cross-platform (Macintosh/IBM) compatibility? This is a nice feature if you are working on more than one platform or have the potential to import data from another platform.

✔ *Cut/Paste:* Does the program support quick and easy cut and paste between entry fields and note fields? This is an important time saver. For example, if you find a source that lists several members of a family with their birth dates, you will want to record the source in the notes field for each individual. It is a lot easier to copy and paste that information than retype it for each person.

✔ *Database Capacity:* Does the program support multiple databases? If you import a database from a source, and want to verify content before adding the data to your main database, make sure the program supports multiple databases.

✔ *Date format:* Is the input format for dates standardized (i.e., 04 July 1776) or does the program allow the user to select the date format? This is a personal preference issue. I like the format that forces all dates to follow dd/mmm/yyyy. It does avoid confusion. Others may want to select their own style.

✔ *Documentation:* Does the program provide space to document every piece of information gathered and prompt the user to add notes? This is critical to good genealogical research. Don't buy a program without it.

✔ *Ease of use:* Is the program easy to learn and easy to use (user friendly) with on-screen helps? Don't buy a piece of software that isn't easy to use. If you accidentally buy a program you don't like, buy another one you do like. Don't spend years of aggravation on a piece of software just because you don't want to discard it.

✔ *Editing:* Is it easy to edit individuals, families, and notes? Genealogists spend a lot of time editing their databases. If editing is difficult or cumbersome, try another program.

✔ *Errors:* How does the program deal with potential errors in data? Does it flag possible problems, or does it give you a list when you ask for one? A good program will help identify possible data entry errors by telling you if a person died before she was born, or if she was ten when the first child was born.

✔ *Evidence:* Does the program help you weigh each piece of evidence for credibility and reliability? This is a good feature, especially if you are very particular about the data that gets added to the database.

✔ *Family order:* Is it easy to rearrange order of children? If you add new children to a family record you often have to rearrange their order. This is a worthwhile feature, but not at the top of the list.

✔ *Fields:* Does the program provide for user-defined fields or dedicated fields for other data such as religion, nationality, languages spoken, Social Security Number, common name, aliases, etc.? This is an interesting feature, and it may be nice to have it. But, it may not be essential. Are the fields flexible enough to support aliases, nicknames, long names, nationality, interest level in various fields? It is sometimes frustrating to be limited to a few spaces to record a name like "de Roquefort-Reynolds."

✔ *Files:* Are the data files interchangeable with other programs? You might want this if you use more than one program or think you might want to change to another software program in the future.

✔ *Footnotes:* Is it easy to include footnotes, print them on family group sheets, or customize the way they appear? Footnotes are important. They should be easy to record and manipulate with the data.

✔ *GEDCOM:* Is the program GEDCOM compatible? The GEDCOM feature allows you to share information with others using files in GEDCOM format. It allows you to copy all or part of your data for exchange. This feature has to be at the top of everyone's list.

✔ *Graphics:* Will it store video and audio recordings, pictures, drawings and scanned images? Computers are now able to deal with graphics fairly easily. It may be nice to have your grandfather's picture on his family group sheet. This is a nice feature that is commonly available, but it is not essential.

✔ *Import/Export:* Does the software allow for the importing and exporting of data from or to another program? This is absolutely essential. If you can't import data you will have to re-key everything you get from someone else. *(See GEDCOM)*

✔ *Internet:* Does the program support direct Internet access back and forth between the program and the Internet? This is a great feature if you are connected to the Internet. If you aren't connected today, you probably will be some day.

✔ *LDS TempleReady:* Is the program compatible with LDS Temple Ready®, and have LDS temple ordinance fields as an option? If you are a member of The Church of Jesus Christ of Latter-day Saints and you are doing your genealogy to submit for temple work, this feature is absolutely essential. For others it is optional.

✔ *Manual:* Does the program have a printed manual as well as an online manual? Online helps are always useful for beginners, but the manuals may be easier to use and contain more detail.

✔ *Match/Merge:* Does the program include automatic, semi-automatic, and manual match and merge? This feature allows you to bring up records for two individuals and compare them side by side to determine if they are the same person. The software should permit you to merge them into one record if they match. This is an essential function for any program if you plan to import any records and link them to the database. Automatic match/merge is a real time saver if you use only a name and an identification number. Semi-automatic allows the genealogist the opportunity to decide if the two records for two individuals should be merged.

✔ *Notes:* What features does the program have for creating, organizing, storing and manipulating notes? Since notes are an essential part of documenting research, the ease for creating and repeating notes is important.

✔ *Parents:* Does the program allow for multiple sets of parents? Sometimes researchers do not agree on the parentage of a person. It is a good idea to record all versions until the correct information has been determined.

✔ *Photos:* Does the program allow for photos in standard digital formats to be linked to the database? It is nice to put photos on printed family group sheets. *(See Graphics)*

✔ *Printing:* What do the printouts look like? This is an important consideration. No matter how sophisticated the program may be, if you don't like the way the printouts look, you won't be happy with it.

✔ *Prompts:* Are there screen prompts to remind the user to link individuals, create notes, add notes to the research log, correct spelling, etc., at the point of data entry? Standardizing entry for dates, places and events will eliminate errors.

✔ *Publishing:* What book publishing capabilities does the program include? Researchers who spend thousands of hours gathering data about their family often want to share it with others. Publishing a book is a good possibility.

✔ *Reports:* What reports can be generated? Reports should include at least the following: ancestor, descendant, pedigree, family group sheets, Ahnentafel report (ancestor table), possible problems, and some custom lists. Some programs have report wizards that help create reports.

✔ *Search:* What are the search capabilities of the program? Does the search feature include browsing capabilities? When you search for an individual in a large database, you need to be able to browse a list of names for other clues that might help identify the object of the search.

✔ *Sources:* How are sources identified, managed, and recorded? It is nice to be able to link a note to a source with a single word and attach the full reference to the note without having to retype the entire bibliographic record.

✔ *Spell Checker:* Does the program include a spell checker? This is a nice feature if you plan to publish your genealogy in a book or on the Internet, but don't reject the program if it otherwise meets your needs. If you are going to publish your genealogy, you will probably put it into a more powerful word processor and check the spelling there.

✔ *Web page Creator:* Does the program provide for the creation of a Web page in Hyper Text Markup Language (HTML) format? This is a very nice feature if you plan to publish your genealogy on the Internet, but there are separate programs that will do the same thing, maybe better.

✔ *Word Processing:* Can you export a report to a word processor? This is a good feature to have if you plan to publish your genealogy.

I know this is a long list, but at least it gives you several important points to consider before buying software. There is also a good book on the subject of genealogical software: Przecha, Donna, and Joan Lowrey. ***Guide to Genealogy Software.*** Baltimore: Genealogical Publishing, 1993. ISBN 080631382X. ∎ *Make sure you get the latest edition.*

Making a List of Features

Making a list of what you think you want is a good idea, but what if you don't know enough about genealogical software to know what you want? The best thing to do is get on the Internet and check out the Web sites for the programs that have them. Browse through the features touted by the producers of each program. Read what others have said about each program. Get a demonstration copy of the program, if they offer a free or low-cost copy. Try out the software. Then make the list of features you want. Use the checklist to decide which features you think you can't live without and look for the program that best matches your requirements. Contact the developers if you still have questions or reservations. Then make your purchase.

Available Genealogical Software

Ancestors and Descendants ®   is a set of computer programs, along with a set of superb instructions for their use. The program lets users create and maintain the genealogical database (or set of databases). The company claims fast and easy correction of any field and instant, automatic error detection on most fields. The pop-up, context-sensitive, help screens show the valid entries in alphabetical order which automatically fills in the field once the entry is selected. This software is easy to learn and use.

Many professional genealogists like Ancestors and Descendants because of its sophisticated features. It can help produce creditable family histories. Although it has numerous colorful bells and whistles, its best attraction is the way it helps avoid tedious and repetitive data-entry tasks, and misleading options not acceptable to the genealogical community. Source recording and management are mature features for this genealogical software. The program offers over one hundred standard reports, including ancestor charts, descendant reports, family group sheets, and statistical reports.

Adventures In Ancestry, Inc., 10714 Hepburn Circle, Culver City, CA 90232-3717
Toll Free: 800-237-5333. International number: 001-310-842-7442
URL: http://www.AIA-AnD.com/ *(Accessed 2/2/98)*

Ancestral Quest ®

by Incline Software is a genealogy software program for Windows that interfaces with PAF (Personal Ancestral File). It is totally compatible with a PAF (Personal Ancestral File) database. Add-on programs and utilities designed for the PAF database can be used with the data from Ancestral Quest. AQ will create a PAF database if one is not already available. Users say that this program has a very intuitive user interface and that it is very easy to learn. The ability to incorporate visuals is a plus. Incline sells a demo disk with a coupon worth $5 off the purchase of the product. Ancestral Quest was rated #1 by *Everton's Genealogical Helper* in May/June 1996.

Ancestral Quest, Incline Software, P.O. Box 17788, Salt Lake City, UT 84117-0778
Toll Free: 800-825-8864. Fax: 801-273-1535.
URL: http://www.ieighty.net/~ancquest/ *(Updated 11/22/97) (Accessed 1/30/98)*

Brothers Keeper for Windows®

by John Steed is a shareware genealogy program that has many of the features of a commercial program including the ability to incorporate pictures. It can import and export GEDCOM files. For notes it can use the built-in editor or jump to any other word processor.

Brother's Keeper Software, 6907 Childsdale Ave., Rockford, MI 49341
Email: 75745.1371@compuserve.com. BBS: 616-364-1127. Fax: 616-866-3345

Cumberland Family Tree® for Windows by Cumberland Family Software. Shareware Version 2.03. It exports and imports GEDCOM files. Each individual can have up to 250 events. In addition, a note can be attached to each event which can be up to 32,000 characters.

Cumberland Family Software, 385 Idaho Springs Rd., Clarksville, TN 37043
Tel: 615-647-4012
URL: http://www.download.com/PC/Result/Download/0,21,0-15771,00.html
  (Free download)

Family Origins® 6.0 for Windows by Parson's. "Recording your family history is as easy as filling in the blanks!" That is what the producers of Family Origins for Windows say. New features include: a photo family tree, super simple data entry, and instant relationship calculator. Other features include family group view, in addition to a pedigree chart as a main program data entry screen, easy-to-use search features, backup/restore built into the program, space for notes for each event, print review, source manager, and an allowance for multiple sets of parents for each individual. Can be ordered and downloaded online.

Parsons Technology, One Parsons Dr., PO Box 100, Hiawatha, IA 52233-0100
Tel: (Main Office): 1-319-395-9626. (Orders): 1-800-223-6925
URL: http://www.parsonstech.com/software/famorig.html *(Accessed 2/2/98)*

Family Treasures®, Family History Software, Master Edition for Windows by Family Technologies has an exceptional tree editor which lets you move freely around your database. Genealogists can add individuals anywhere in the tree. The program handles unlimited spouses and up to 40 children per family. Adoptions and special relationships are no problem. Each family member can have an unlimited biography and medical data with suppression for sensitive data. Family Treasures is a superior program for storing and printing graphics.

Family Treasures, Family Technologies, P.O. Box 309, Westfield, NY 14787-0309 Tel: 716-792-9679. Email: 71543.2760@compuserve.com.

URL: http://www.famtech.com/fa00001.htm *(Accessed 2/2/98)*

Family Tree Maker Deluxe CD-ROM®, 3.0 by Broderbund is easy to use and comprehensive. *The Family Finder Index,* now on two CDs, lists more than 130 million people whose names appear in centuries of historical records and identifies which CDs contain information on the ancestor. The graphics feature imports Kodak Photo CD, BMP, TIFF, and OLE objects. Family Tree Maker is compatible with GEDCOM and PAF formats. Uses *Family Finder Index* which can also be used to search *Family Archives CD's* available from Family Tree Maker. Family Tree Maker now has a vast online community and new features make finding ones family even easier.

URL: http://www.familytreemaker.com/ *(Accessed 2/2/98).* Available from many genealogical suppliers and over the Internet.

The Master Genealogist (TMG)®, DOS 1.2a by Wholly Genes, Inc. Is a flexible tool for genealogists. It is easy for the novice to understand, learn, and use. It can also meet the needs of the professional. TMG can accommodate every piece of data you want to record and is limited only by the capacity of the hard drive. Version 1.2a provides many reports including register, modified register, and reverse register. It will also generate the elements of a book including a table of contents, footnotes/ endnotes, multiple indexes, and bibliography. It also supports output directly to the native format of more than 50 word processors.

Wholly Genes, 6868 Ducketts Ln., Elk Ridge, MD, 21227
Tel: Technical Support: 410-796-2447. Orders: 1-800-982-2103
URL: http://www.WhollyGenes.com/ *(Updated: 2/1/98) (Accessed 2/2/98)*

Personal Ancestral File ™ 3.0 is the latest version of the standard on which Family History is based. This program was developed by The Church of Jesus Christ of Latter-day Saints to help its members record and organize their genealogy and submit names for temple work. It is designed to record genealogical information, organize data into family groups and pedigrees, identify areas where additional research is needed, and keep track of information sources and the information they provided. Also the ability to search records, print standard or custom-designed reports and merge/match duplicate records in your files. The Genealogical Information Exchange Feature allows the user to share information with others using files in GEDCOM format. $15.

Salt Lake Distribution Center, 1999 W 1700 South, Salt Lake, UT 84014-4233
Tel: Orders: 800-537-5950 (Have credit card ready). 801-240-2584. (Canada: 800-453-3860 ext. 203)

PAF Windows Companion

The Family History Department is releasing Personal Ancestral File Companion for home use. It works with PAF 3.0 and will help home users print quality genealogy charts and reports with a Windows-supported printer. The PAF Windows Companion is available for $10 from the Salt Lake Distribution Center.

Salt Lake Distribution Center, 1999 W 1700 South, Salt Lake, UT 84014-4233
Tel: Orders: 800-537-5950 (Have credit card ready). 801-240-2584. (Canada: 800-453-3860 ext. 203)

Reunion 5® for Macintosh

by Leister Productions, Inc. is a top-rated genealogical tool for the Macintosh. Reunion helps the genealogist document, store, and display genealogy information, notes, sources, pictures, sounds, and videos. It displays family relationships in an artistic, graphic form. Reunion makes publishing genealogical information and sharing it on the Internet easy. Common reports are created automatically. Reunion calculates relationships, ages, and life expectancies. And it includes GEDCOM import/export capabilities. The program is fully GEDCOM compatible and lets the user transfer data or exchange data with others—even those who use other genealogical software. Reunion offers a free demonstration version that can be downloaded off the Internet.

Leister Productions, Inc., PO Box 289, Mechanicsburg, PA 17055
Tel: 717-697-1378. Fax: 717-697-4373 . Technical Support: help@LeisterPro.com.
Information: info@LeisterPro.com.
URL: http://www.LeisterPro.com/ *(Accessed 2/2/98)*
Reunion for Windows has been acquired by Sierra.

Ultimate Family Tree® by Palladium is an easy-to-use and powerful genealogy program. The step-by-step instructions make it easy to get started, and it will save weeks of research time. This top-rated software has been well reviewed by computer magazines. Ultimate Family Tree is capable of handling 350 million names. It includes the Social Security Death Index which includes over 54 million names. The Family Tutor uses multimedia features to enhance the programs flexibility. It is helpful for the beginner genealogist because its Records Requester instantly generates letters needed for information and statistics. Ultimate Family Tree, available for Macintosh and PC platforms, is available in three versions.

Paladium Interactive. Tel: 812-829-4405. Sales: 800-910-2696.
Email: pisupport@aol.com
URL: http://www.uftree.com/ *(Accessed 2/2/98)*

Selecting a Genealogy Software Program

In the class I teach for the Great Bend Recreation Commission, students often ask me which genealogy software program they should buy. I try not to recommend any specific one, but rather give class members several choices. In 1990, I purchased Personal Ancestral File when it was the least expensive software and one of the few on the market. Today, I use Ancestral Quest, primarily because my wife's cousin gave it to us as a gift. Both programs are very functional, and they use the same database.

Summary

While careful study and comparison is important, any genealogy software is so much better than keeping records the old way, that most people really like whatever they select. It is much better than keeping their genealogy manually. There is little chance of making a mistake that can't be remedied by buying another program. Data from most programs can be imported into the new one. Remember that cheap isn't always bad and costly isn't always best.

Chapter 8

Using Computers–Genealogy & the Internet

*T*he proliferation of genealogy information and resources on the Internet is so rapid and vast that no one seems to be able to keep up with it. One of the major advantages of this development is the immediacy of access. I used to think that genealogy was for older people because they were the only ones with enough patience to spend hours looking at a roll of microfilm or waiting for weeks the get a response in the mail. The Internet eliminates this delay. Databases, online services, online card catalogs, and email have changed the way we get information. Instead of waiting weeks and months, we can send messages back and forth several times in one day. Genealogists who faced frustrating challenges in the past are now are online, helping others.

To aid librarians and others who have access to the Internet, I have compiled the following list of the Web sites I would highly recommend. Some, like Cyndi Howells' site, you would probably find without looking very hard. Others are more obscure, and I have included them because they are unique. URLs change every day, but genealogy Web sites rarely go away; they just move. If one or more of the URLs on the list doesn't take you to the Web site I have listed, try searching for the title of the Web site using one of the search engines like Alta Vista. The site has probably just moved to a new location.

Genealogy Sites on the Internet

The Biggest

Cyndi's List of Genealogy Sites on the Internet   This resource has the most links (over 30,000) to genealogical resources. It is constantly updated and the links are categorized and cross-referenced. Cyndi has put a lot of work into making this site user friendly. It is perfect for the beginning genealogist and anyone else who uses the Internet to do research. Cyndi is also the author of *Netting Your Ancestors* (p. 105), an excellent book on using the Internet for genealogical research.
URL: http://www.cyndilist.com *(Updated 2/1/98) (Accessed 2/2/98)*

Best Genealogy Links on the WWW   This is a listing of the top genealogy sites on the Internet, with links to each site. The annotations give a brief description of each Web site and make it easy to discover what information can be found by accessing the site.
URL: http://www.geocities.com/Heartland/1637/ *(Updated: 1/3/1998) (Accessed 2/2/98)*

Digital Librarian: A Librarian's Choice of the Best on the Web—Genealogy   This is a long list of Web sites on genealogy. The one-line descriptions are sufficient to help you decide whether or not you want to visit the sites.
URL: http://www.servtech.com/public/mvail/genealogy.html *(Accessed 2/2/98)*

The U.S. GenWeb Project This is a database developed by volunteers that provides a single entry point to genealogical databases for all states and counties in the United States. Volunteer specialists in each county may be queried via email. It is a very ambitious project.
URL: http://www.usgenweb.com/ *(Accessed 2/2/98)*

For Beginners

Beginner's Guide to Family History Research "If you can't even spell the word g-e-n-e-a-l-o-g-y, this is the place for you to start." This is how this site for beginners created by Desmond Walls Allen and Carolyn Earle Billingsley opens. This extensive, well-written piece has all the steps any beginner would need to get started.
URL: http://biz.ipa.net/arkresearch/guide.html *(Accessed 2/2/98)*

Family History Information: How Do I Begin? This Web site answers the questions: *Why family history? Why do members of The Church of Jesus Christ of Latter-day Saints do family history research? What can I do first? What is a Family History Center? Where is the nearest Family History Center?* The answers, which are just a click away, give beginners a good start on their research.
URL: http://lds.org/Family_History/How_Do_I_Begin.html *(Accessed 2/2/98)*

Family Tree Maker How-to Guide This is a great way to begin family research. It has addresses and information about archives and libraries that all researchers will find helpful. It includes step-by-step instructions for locating family information and forms to facilitate research.
URL: http://www.familytreemaker.com/mainmenu.html *(Accessed 2/2/98)*

The Genealogy Home Page This is another perfect site for the beginner. It is the ultimate page for beginning genealogists, with guides, libraries, software, maps and geography. Sponsored by Family Tree Maker.
URL: http://www.genhomepage.com/ *(Updated 1/27/98) (Accessed 2/2/98)*

Genealogy Online I would consider this a "must see" site with unique links to genealogy chat rooms and other online databases. It offers email forwarding, a sample of the online 1880 census, a catalog of microfilmed census schedules, the Emcee Internet Directory, all home pages for Genealogy Online, a list of genealogy bulletin boards (BBS) and a genealogy events calendar, Soundex conversion.
URL: http://www.genealogy.org/ *(Updated 1/26/98) (Accessed 2/2/98)*

Getting Started in Genealogy – Connecticut State Library This site is maintained by the Connecticut State Library, and it is an excellent site for anyone who is just getting started with family history research. Besides some nice Connecticut links, it has a good list of "how-to" books and some good ideas for beginners. It offers a great opening page; everything fits on one screen.
URL: http://www.cslnet.ctstateu.edu/starting.htm *(Accessed 2/2/98)*

Seven Steps to a Family Tree: A Beginners Guide to Genealogy This online guide presents the seven basic steps in tracing an American family tree. Following the steps is the beginning of a pilgrimage into the past. This guide ably shows the beginner how it's done.
URL: http://www.agll.com/trivia/7steps.html *(Accessed 2/2/98)*

Search Engines

Genealogist's Index to the World Wide Web The Genealogist's Index to the World Wide Web is maintained by Eastern Digital Resources. They feature surname folders on more than 2,000 different surnames.
URL: http://members.aol.com/genwebindx/index.htm *(Updated 1/8/98) (Accessed 2/2/98)*

I Found It! Genealogy Search Engine   This is a directory of genealogy-related sites on the World Wide Web. Search criteria are compared to the information about the site. You can type in any genealogical terms to search the genealogy directory. The site is useful for searching surnames, genealogical terms or sources. Only identified genealogy sites are included.
URL: http://www.gensource.com/ifoundit/index.htm *(Accessed 2/2/98)*

Kentucky Vital Records Index   This data was acquired from Kentucky's State Office of Vital Statistics for non-commercial use only. Files contain an index to deaths which have been registered in Kentucky from 1 January 1911 to 31 December 1992. Information includes the name of the deceased, date of death, age at death, and county of death and of residence. This is an excellent search engine for Kentucky deaths. Indexes for marriages and divorces are also available at this site.
URL: http://ukcc.uky.edu/~vitalrec/ *(Accessed 2/2/98)*

NARA Archival Information Locator (NAIL)   A pilot database of selected holdings in the National Archives, NAIL is a searchable database that contains information about a wide variety of the holdings of the National Archives and Records Administration across the country. Researchers can use NAIL to search descriptions for key words or topics, and then to retrieve digital copies of selected textual documents, photographs, maps, and sound recordings.
URL: http://www.nara.gov/nara/nail.html *(Updated: 12/10/97) (Accessed 2/2/98)*

Roots Surname List — Interactive Search   One of the first, and still one of my favorite sites. The Roots Surname List (RSL) is a list or registry of 200,000 surnames submitted by 20,000+ genealogists. Associated with each surname are dates and locations, and information about how to contact the person who submitted the surname. Researchers working on the same family, in the same area and in a similar time frame can contact each other and share information via email or regular mail. I have found several distant cousins using the RSL. The following sample entry from the list shows how the information is presented. It is further explained on p. 27.

Swan   1600   now   MA>CT>Albany Co., NY>IL> AZ>CA, USA   jswan

URL: http://www.rootsweb.com/rootsweb/searches/rslsearch.html *(Accessed 2/2/98)*

Yahoo Genealogy Page   Yahoo, the well-known search engine on the Internet, has a page just for genealogists. It has links to the more important genealogy sites and is a good starting point for beginners.
URL: http://www.acpl.lib.in.us/Genealogy/Getting_Started_Index.html
(Updated 5/14/97) (Accessed 2/2/98)

Directories

Directory of Genealogy Libraries in the U.S.   This is a very long list of libraries that have genealogical research materials. It gives the name and address of the library.
URL: http://www.greenheart.com/rdietz/gen_libs.htm *(Accessed 2/2/98)*

FuneralNet Directory   There are over 20,000 U.S. funeral homes listed on this site. You can search by: funeral home name, address, city, county, or state. Results will give you name, address, telephone number, and fax (if available). In a town with only a few funeral homes, one or two telephone calls could yield the information you need.
URL: http://www.funeralnet.com/search.html *(Accessed 2/2/98)*

The LDS Meeting House Locator Data Provided by Yahoo Yellow Pages™   In two steps you can find the location and telephone number of the nearest LDS meeting house. You start by finding the city and state and then the name of the church. I found the FHC in Great Bend, Kansas, which is not listed in the previous site.
URL: http://www.deseretbook.com/locate/front.html *(Accessed 2/2/98)*

Repositories of Primary Sources   If you want to know which archives and libraries have major collections of primary source documents, check this Web site. It lists over 2,400 other Web sites which describe the holdings of manuscripts, archives, rare books, historical photographs, and other primary sources.
URL: http://www.uidaho.edu/special-collections/Other.Repositories.html
(Updated 1/98) (Accessed 2/2/98)

Where Is the Nearest Family History Center™?   This site gives state-by-state telephone numbers of Local Family History Centers. Not all FHCs are given on this list. They still suggest contacting a local LDS congregation, preferably on a Sunday, or contacting Family History Support at 1-800-346-6044 for the nearest FHC.
URL: http://lds.org/Family_History/Where_is.html *(Accessed 2/2/98)*

Mailing Lists

 Genealogy Listservs, Newsgroups, and Special Home Pages   This is a list of mail list groups or listservs on the Internet that may be of value to genealogists. Listservs allow researchers with similar interests to join together and share information common to them. The focus of the group may be for a particular surname or region of the country, a state or county. The site has a convenient search engine.
URL: http://www.eskimo.com/~chance/ *(Accessed 2/2/98)*

Genealogy Resources on the Internet—Mailing Lists   This is John Fuller's page on mailing lists. The mailing lists linked to this site are divided into five categories: 1) general mailing lists; 2) software; 3) non-USA geographic areas; 4) United States, arranged by state; and 5) surnames arranged alphabetically. This site describes the scope of each mailing list and tells how to subscribe.
URL: http://members.aol.com/johnf14246/gen_mail.html *(Accessed 2/2/98)*

Listserv.Northwest.Com—U.S. County Lists   At this site you can subscribe to a genealogy mailing list for any county in the United States. Once you are on the list, you can post a message to the list and then look for responses.
URL: http://listserv.northwest.com/~haight/countylist.htm *(Accessed 2/2/98)*

Roots-L Home Page   Roots-L started in 1987 as a mailing list. Today it has over 7,000 subscribers. If you want a lot of email and have a large mail box, or if you have several lines you are actively researching at the same time, subscribe to Roots-L, but don't lose the opening message that tells you how to unsubscribe.
URL: http://www.rootsweb.com/roots-l/ *(Accessed 2/2/98)*

User Mailing Lists Hosted by RootsWeb   User Mailing Lists Hosted by RootsWeb offers links to mailing lists, with instructions for subscribers. Mailing lists are a good way to find other researchers who may have information to share.
URL: http://www.rootsweb.com/~maillist/ *(Accessed 2/2/98)*

Commercial Sites

Ancestry Search-Database Searching   Although it is a commercial site, it offers lots of free access to information and is one of the best research tools on the Internet. This includes over 51 million searchable Social Security records and American marriage records, the largest collection of searchable marriage records on the Web.
URL: http://www.ancestry.com/ *(Accessed 2/2/98)*

Everton Publishers   This is a another helpful commercial site for beginners. It features links to a catalog of products and services, archives and libraries, and other resources, including online publications, software reviews and online BBS services.
URL: http://www.everton.com/ *(Accessed 2/2/98)*

Family Tree Maker Online   This commercial site for genealogists offers interviews

with noted genealogists. You can also find out about local and national genealogical organizations and societies, and search the FamilyFinder Index online, free! This directory lists 115 million names from centuries of census and marriage indexes, birth records, actual family trees, and other resources.
URL: http://www.familytreemaker.com/ *(Accessed 2/2/98)*

Heritage Quest, AGLL Genealogical Services   Heritage Quest is a commercial site with access to free information resources. It is sponsored by America's largest family history provider. They rent microfilm to members and institutions. Among the features of this site is the online guide: *Seven Steps to a Family Tree: A Beginners Guide to Genealogy.*
URL: http://www.agll.com/ *(Accessed 2/2/98)*

Adoption

Starting a Search for Birth Parents or Birth Family   Searching for birth parents or a child given up for adoption can be time consuming and stressful. Much of the information here is for searching adoptees, but there is also information on searching for relinquished children and long-lost relatives. This site has good step-by-step instructions and helpful links.
URL:http://www.pcis.net/colleen/search1a.htm *(Accessed 2/2/98)*

Handwritng

Deciphering Old Handwriting   Reading the handwriting on original documents can be difficult without help. The information at this site comes from a course taught by Sabina J. Murray. It is worth a look for anyone who has to read old documents.
URL: http://www.firstct.com/fv/oldhand.html *(Accessed 2/2/98)*

National Membership Organizations

GenServ - Family History   The first requirement for subscription to this Web site, which is maintained by Cliff Manis, is a GEDCOM of the subscriber's personal family history. The system is based on sharing family information. They have 10,000+ databases and over fourteen million individual members. The regular annual subscription fee is $12/year with a discount to $6/year for senior citizens (over sixty) and students. There are other levels of access. One of the major differences in GenServ over other systems is that the GEDCOM file itself is protected and never released in GEDCOM format. Subscribers query the system and receive reports. The GEDCOMs will never be sold on CD or given away. I have used this service with great success.
URL: http://www.genserv.com/ *(Accessed 2/2/98)*

National Genealogical Society   The National Genealogical Society is a national membership organization with 14,000+ members. Their site contains charts, forms, aids, and special reference materials. Members can search the society's online catalog and borrow materials from it. They have a 30,000 volume collection and circulate most of these titles to their members via UPS and USPS.
URL: http://www.genealogy.org/~ngs/ *(Accessed 2/2/98)*

Regional Sites

Hacker's Creek Pioneer Descendants   The Hacker's Creek Pioneer Descendants is an organization dedicated to the history and genealogy of West Virginia, concentrating on central West Virginia, and Lewis, Harrison, Monongalia, Barbour, Upshur, Webster, Braxton, Gilmer, and Doddridge Counties. This is an example of a regional site where local volunteers have done a good job of gathering genealogical information about an area and mounting it on the Internet.
URL: http://www.rootsweb.com/~hcpd/ *(Updated 1/11/98) (Accessed 2/2/98)*

Traveller Southern Families   This Web site concentrates on southern families. You will find family trees donated by individuals, a Web bulletin board service, and Internet references to hundreds of other excellent Web sites containing valuable genealogical information.

URL: http://genealogy.traveller.com/genealogy/ *(Accessed 2/2/98)*

Custom Publishers

Evagean Publishing   This company will publish, market and distribute your genealogy at no cost to you. The cost of publication is covered by book sales. They have a pre-publication process that accurately predicts the demand for the work and guarantees commercial success. They reserve the right to decline any project they deem not to be viable.

URL: http://webnz.com/evagean/ *(Accessed 2/2/98)*

Genealogy Publishing Service   This publishing company provides complete service for the preparation and typesetting of camera-ready manuscripts and publishing of all types of genealogical and historical books. GPC and their subsidiaries have published more than 5,000 titles in genealogy and related fields.

URL: http://www.intertekweb.com/gpsbook/ *(Updated 11/13/97)* *(Accessed 2/2/98)*

Genealogical Publishers

Ancestor Publishers   This publisher produces both microfiche and books. It offers a wide selection of microfiche for both historians and genealogists. It is a low-cost way to get genealogical material.

URL: http://www.firstct.com/fv/ancpub.html *(Accessed 2/2/98)*

Genealogical Publishing Company   The is the electronic home of Genealogical Publishing Company, Inc., the largest commercial publisher of genealogical reference books, textbooks, and how-to books in the world. GPC and their subsidiaries have published more than 5,000 titles in genealogy and related fields.

URL: http://www.genealogical.com/ *(Accessed 2/2/98)*

Higginson Book Company   Higginson is a major reprinter of genealogies and local histories. This could be a good source for materials that are unavailable from other sources.

URL: http://www.higginsonbooks.com/ *(Accessed 2/2/98)*

Iberian Publishing Company's Online Genealogy   A publisher of genealogical materials specializing in reference works for genealogists and historians researching the Virginias and other southeastern states, 1650–1850.

URL: http://www.iberian.com/ *(Accessed 2/2/98)*

Tennessee Valley Publishing (TVP)   Tennessee Valley Publishing (TVP) is a subsidy press that assists individuals (especially family historians) and organizations in documenting and publishing their books.

URL: http://pw1.netcom.com/~tvp1/index.htm *(Accessed 2/2/98)*

UMI Research Collections - Genealogy and Local History   UMI's Genealogy and Local History program provides a unique, ongoing collection of research materials for tracing family lineages, beginning with the thirteen original colonies. This extensive microfiche collection can meet the needs of all genealogists—amateurs and professionals alike. It gives them access to documents that might otherwise be inaccessible. For the benefit of individuals, titles from the first 30 units are available for single-title sale.

URL: http://www.umi.com/hp/Support/Research/Files/324.html *(Accessed 2/2/98)*

Ethnic Sites

Christine's Genealogy Web Site   This is Christine Cheryl Charity's comprehensive collection of African American genealogical resources. It features lots of links to other sites and is an excellent source on African American research.
URL: http://ccharity.com/ *(Updated 2/1/98) (Accessed 2/2/98)*

Hispanic Genealogical Society   This is a good place to start a search for Hispanic ancestors. They offer databases on families of northern Mexico, south Texas, California, and New Mexico. It has hundreds of links to other Hispanic genealogy sites.
URL: http://www.brokersys.com/~joguerra/jose.html *(Updated 12/23/97) (Accessed 2/2/98)*

JewishGen: The Home of Jewish Genealogy   This site features a discussion group, information files, searchable databases, special interest groups, and much more. This is a great beginning point for genealogists of Jewish ancestry.
URL: http://www.jewishgen.org/ *(Updated 1/19/98) (Accessed 2/2/98)*

Native American Genealogy   This site has many links to other Native American genealogy sites. It is a good springboard to more specific types of information.
URL: http://members.aol.com/bbbenge/front.html *(Accessed 2/2/98)*

General

ALA/Reference and User Services Association, History Section   This section of ALA/RUSA represents the subject interests of reference librarians, genealogists, archivists, bibliographers, historians, and others engaged in historical reference or research. The Genealogy Committee provides a forum to advance the interests of librarians who serve genealogical researchers. The committee regularly sponsors an ALA pre-conference entitled "Reference Service for Genealogists: A Mini-Course for Librarians."
URL: http://weber.u.washington.edu/~mudrock/HIST/ *(Updated 1/21/98) (Accessed 2/2/98)*

Database of Illinois Civil War Veterans   This is a searchable database of Civil War veterans from Illinois. It is from a 1900-1901 publication that originated from the rosters maintained during the Civil War by the Illinois Adjutant General. The names of approximately 250,000 men, organized into 175 regiments, are found on this database.
URL: http://www.sos.state.il.us/depts/archives/datcivil.html *(Updated 9/22/97)*
(Accessed 2/2/98)

Genealogy Toolbox   Surname data in this resource is listed alphabetically. The Surname Query list is easy to browse. A Genealogy Site Submission page allows individuals to submit their new site to several major genealogy indexes. A group of searchable index pages allow users to directly search other collections without having to go to each individual site.
URL: http://genealogy.tbox.com/ *(Accessed 2/2/98)*

Genealogy's Most Wanted   Find the surnames and known information on a person that is "MOST WANTED." Researchers may submit information requests to this site, and this can often lead to responses from other researchers who have worked on that family line. The researcher's email address or their snail mail address is provided in case someone has information. An average of 50 new names appear daily.
URL: http://www.citynet.net/mostwanted/ *(Updated 1/29/98) (Accessed 2/2/98)*

Irene's Genealogy Resources   This site offers links to genealogy resources in five categories: books, graveyards, help resources, look-ups and research resources. It contains a good section on using the U. S. Federal Census.
URL: http://www.thecore.com/~hand/genealogy/links/resource.html *(Accessed 2/2/98)*

Journal of Online Genealogy   The Journal is a free e-zine which focuses on the use of online resources and techniques in genealogy and family history.
URL: http://www.onlinegenealogy.com/ *(Accessed 2/2/98)*

Links to State Archives and Libraries   This list of Web site links to state archives is maintained by the West Virginia State Archives. It is handy for those who want to see what a particular state archive has to offer genealogists.
URL: http://www.wvlc.wvnet.edu/history/linkarch.html *(Accessed 2/2/98)*

RAND Genealogy Club   The RAND Genealogy Club is a group of RAND employees who provide this page to share information about genealogical resources on the "information highway."
URL: http://www.rand.org:80/personal/Genea/^

Root Diggin' Department   There are hundreds of genealogy links relating to Janyce's family and others at this site. Help for newbies and "old timers" too.
URL: http://www.janyce.com/gene/rootdig.html *(Accessed 2/2/98)*

Susan Wedig's Homepage   This is a good example of how someone can put their genealogy on the net. It is simple, easy to interpret, and attractive. I have included it to show genealogists one way they can add their genealogy to the Internet.

Susan says, "Welcome to my genealogy page and see how I'm linked to my West Virginia ancestors. I've divided this list into primary surnames (direct descendants) and secondary surnames (names that married to my direct line). You may click on any underlined ancestor to view known offspring. Let me know if you find a name you recognize or just want to know how I did it! — Susan Wedig."
URL: http://www.strato.net/~wedigs/genealogy.html *(Accessed 2/2/98)*

Where to Find It—Records Selection Table   This handy table tells you where to look first if you need a certain kind of data; then where to search if you can't find it in the first place you check.
URL: http://www.rootsweb.com/~mimecost/where.html *(Accessed 2/2/98)*

Getting Help from Other Librarians

There is a good group of librarians on the Internet: Librarians Serving Genealogists. Their Web site has links to libraries that have significant genealogical collections. See http://www.cas.usf.edu/lis/genealib/ *(Updated 1/11/98)* *(Accessed 1/30/98)*. They have a mailing list known as GENEALIB, for announcements, discussion, and question-and-answers of interest to genealogy librarians. If you have access to email, join the group. To subscribe, send an email message to: listserv@nosferatu.cas.usf.edu. Leave the subject line blank (if your email system does not allow you to leave the subject line blank, then put only a period in it). In the body of the message, put only: subscribe genealib Yourfirstname Yourlastname.

There is also a section in the American Library Association, RUSA, for librarians who serve genealogists—ALA/Reference and User Services Association, History Section (http://weber.u.washington.edu/~mudrock/HIST/) *(Updated 1/29/98)* *(Accessed 1/29/98)*

If you are a member of ALA you might want to align yourself with this group for additional assistance with genealogical reference. They also sponsor regular preconferences for genealogical reference librarians.

Book Reviews

Here are a few more books on computers and genealogy that might be useful in a library.

Bonner, Laurie, and Steve Bonner. *Searching for Cyber-Roots: A Step-by-Step Guide to Genealogy on the World Wide Web.* Salt Lake City: Ancestry, 1997. ISBN: 0916489787 (softcover) ☎

All over the world genealogists are sharing their genealogy with the lightening speed of the Internet. Even if you have never touched a computer before, this book will help you become a part of the excitement. This is a good book for the circulating collection or a personal collection.

Cooper, Brian, ed. *The Internet*. New York: DK Publishing, 1996. ISBN: 0789412888.

This is not a genealogy book, but anyone who wants to do genealogical research on the Internet ought to read it. The subtitle for the book is "How to get connected and explore the World Wide Web, exchange news and email, download software, and communicate on-line." Maybe the full color graphics make me think this is one of the best books available on the topic, but it is also clearly written and easy to understand. It answers questions like: *What is the Internet? How do I get connected? How do you download files? How do you send email? What is the World Wide Web? What are Gopherspace, Telenet, and Newsgroups? What are relay chat rooms?* and *What are Virtual Worlds?*

The appendix has useful information about online services, troubleshooting, common file formats, and a few useful Web page URLs. The glossary has understandable definitions to many Internet terms you probably won't find in a regular dictionary. If you don't have it, get this book for your library.

Cosgriff, John and Carolyn. *Turbo Genealogy: An Introduction to Family History Research in the Information Age.* Salt Lake City: Ancestry, 1997.

This is a genealogical research primer. It outlines the steps and requirements for tracing a family tree. It provides basic instruction for new genealogists or those who are just starting their research.

Secondly, this book is a reference tool that will help beginning researchers take advantage of new research tools. Recent changes in libraries and computer technology can expedite research. This book teaches how to search computer-generated databases.

Thirdly, this book teaches how to effectively use a personal computer to keep track of research, communicate with other researchers, and electronically access information from remote sources.

Some long-standing obstacles to genealogical research are beginning to melt away. Computers are helping topple the "brick walls" which almost inevitably beset individual researchers.

Crowe, Elizabeth Powell. *Genealogy Online: Researching Your Roots.* 2nd ed. New York: McGraw-Hill, 1996. ISBN 0-07-014754-X ■

Online services and the Internet are giving family researchers faster access to genealogical information that could take years to locate using traditional methods. It teaches genealogists how take advantage of the vast amount of genealogical information now available on the electronic super highway.

This easy-to-read guide brings you the latest in useful, new information on the Internet, World Wide Web, and the latest software. It explains how to tap into all the online services and take full advantage of: newsgroups, Web pages, and library online catalogs. It won't teach you how to do genealogy, but it will help you understand how to use the tools of the online world to do it better.

Howells, Cyndi. *Netting Your Ancestors: Genealogical Research on the Internet.* Baltimore, Maryland: Genealogical Publishing, 1997. ISBN: 0-8063-1546-6.

Netting Your Ancestors is designed not only to show you how to use the Internet in genealogical research, but how to take maximum advantage of this extraordinary research tool. Written by genealogist and computer whiz Cyndi Howells, creator of the award-winning Web site Cyndi's List of Genealogy Sites on the Internet, it is a guide to the most powerful research tool since the advent of the personal computer.

With its clear, no-nonsense approach, *Netting Your Ancestors* answers the most fundamental questions about genealogical research on the Internet: *How do I get online? What type of computer hardware and software do I need? What do I do once I'm online? Where do I start? What type of information is available?* The answers to those questions, rendered in plain English, will help you to discover genealogical resources and finding-aids beyond your wildest dreams. What's more, you'll be able to communicate with researchers around the world, exchanging data that otherwise might take you a lifetime to find.

Netting Your Ancestors focuses on the three most useful components of the Internet: email, mailing lists and newsgroups, and the World Wide Web. The last section in each chapter is devoted to research strategies that will benefit both new and veteran online researchers.

The ability to exchange information on a global scale and to explore vast new databases (as well as obscure factoids lurking at the edges of cyberspace) is what genealogical research on the Internet is all about. And in this book, Cyndi Howells starts you out on your Internet journey of exploration and discovery, guiding you confidently toward your goal. It's a trip you'll never forget, even though you never leave home.

Source: Cyndi's List of Genealogy Sites on the Internet *(Reprinted with permission ©* *1997)* http://www.cyndilist.com *(Accessed 2/2/98)*

Kemp, Thomas Jay. **Virtual Roots: A Guide to Genealogy and Local History on the World Wide Web.** Wilmington, Delaware: Scholarly Resources, 1997. ISBN: 0-8420-2718-1(cloth) ISBN 0-8420-2720-3 (paper). ■

There are over 30 million sites on the World Wide Web. This book guides the reader in using the Internet and focuses on the sites that will be most helpful to genealogists and local historians. *Virtual Roots* shows Internet users where to go for answers and what they will find.

This directory lists sites of the best archives, libraries, institutions, genealogical and historical societies, and family associations around the world—the ones that provide census indexes, genealogical data, and bibliographies. *Virtual Roots* gives the URL, email address, complete mailing address, and phone and/or fax numbers. Extraordinary and outstanding sites are noted—a nice touch when you have to decide where to go first. This book is essential for anyone who uses the Internet for genealogical research.

Virtual Roots is an indispensable tool for every library that offers public access to the Internet and genealogical reference service.

Oldfield, Jim. **Your Family Tree Using Your PC.** Grand Rapids, Michigan: Abacus, 1997. ISBN: 1-55755-310-6. 🎓

This book makes good use of graphics to explain how family historians can use their home computers for genealogy. It covers planning research, tools of the trade, where to begin, researching online, using genealogy software, and using the CD-ROM that comes with the book. The appendix has a list of over 2,000 resource facilities. *Your Family Tree Using Your PC* would be most useful in the circulating collection.

Summary

Anyone who tries to do genealogy today without a computer is working hard and not smart. Computers are affordable for most people and all libraries. They should all be hooked up to the Internet if users want to get the most out of their investment. People who come to libraries should find at least one public access computer to use for genealogy, searching the Internet or word processing. Computers are wonderful tools and people should use them to make their work easier.

Chapter 9

Hiring a Professional Researcher

Seeking the help of a professional researcher can be either a first step or a last step. Some people who are just getting into genealogy need someone who knows their way around research facilities to do a survey for them. Others may be at the "end of their rope" and don't know where to turn. Some family researchers with overseas ancestors may not speak or read the language. They may need to turn to a professional in the country of origin for help. In any case hiring someone else to do your genealogical research is not uncommon.

In some cases it may be better to call on a local professional researcher and pay a modest fee, than to spend a thousand dollars or more to travel to the area and do the research yourself. On one occasion my mother traveled from Arizona to Missouri to find information on her great-grandmother. She spent over a thousand dollars and came home empty-handed. Years later I found the information she was looking for through an email connection.

The easiest way to find a professional researcher is through libraries and archives. Every major research facility can probably supply a list of people who will do research for a fee. Even small institutions like local public libraries can probably furnish names and addresses of a few people in the community who will do research. For instance, if a person needed research done in our county, the Great Bend Public Library could provide the names of at least three people who could do research for them.

Main Concerns

The questions most often asked by those who are considering a professional genealogist are:

1. *How much will it cost?*

Most professionals charge between $10 and $25 per hour plus copying and mailing expenses. Many professional genealogists advertise their services in genealogical periodicals like *The Genealogical Helper, Heritage Quest, Forum, Genealogy Bulletin,* and others. Anyone can contact them to determine their fees and their area of expertise.

2. *Can I rely on the information I get?*

Generally, yes, but professional researchers are people and they can make mistakes. Asking for photocopies of original sources whenever possible is one way to verify the information they dig up for you. Make sure they cite their sources and provide a copy of the text they find.

3. *How do I find one I can trust?*

The most important question in hiring a professional genealogist is how to determine if he or she is qualified to do the job you want done. Several organizations accredit or certify researchers. The people on their lists can generally be trusted to do a good job. Your patrons can contact these places for the names of qualified researchers in their area of interest.

When communicating with someone regarding a genealogical service or favor, it is best to send a self-addressed, stamped envelope (SASE). For out-of-country queries, include International Reply Coupons, available at most post offices.

Many professional genealogists are listed through their certifying or accrediting organizations. Contact one or more of the groups listed in this section for a list of their professional genealogists. Have your patron contact the top recommended individuals. If the person they contact lacks the expertise in a particular area of research, he or she will probably be able to make a referral to another researcher who has the appropriate skills.

The genealogist who is hiring a professional needs to ask for their credentials: education, professional affiliations, publications, foreign languages (if relevant), and access to records. If the research involves uncommon problems, ask what experience the professional has in those specialties.

Don't forget to discuss fees in the first query letter. Find out how much they will charge and the method of payment. Some professionals want some money up front and then work on an hourly basis after that. It is a good idea to set a dollar limit with the researcher. It is just good business to have a mutual understanding about your budget before any work is done.

Once the fees are agreed upon, the client and researcher will want to agree on exactly what the researcher is expected to do. This requires letting the researcher know what is wanted. Will he work on only one or two ancestral lines or will he research all of them? Allow the researcher a reasonable amount of time to do the work.

Certifying or Accrediting Organizations

BCG
PO Box 5816
Falmouth, VA 22403-5816
or
P.O. Box 14291
Washington, DC 20044
URL:
http://www.genealogy.org/~bcg/
(Updated 12/697)
(Accessed 2/2/98)

Board for Certification of Genealogists   Founded in 1964, the Board for Certification of Genealogists (BCG) has promoted expertise and high standards among professional genealogists. Board-certified genealogists, whether professionals or highly skilled hobbyists, pass rigorous tests and subscribe to a code of ethics. To ensure that their skills are continually updated, certified genealogists are reevaluated every five years. The Board has developed specific and discriminating examinations in six categories. BCG is independent of any society, although its trustees and judges are always national leaders in the field.

The Roster of Board Certified Genealogist is available from the Board. It details qualifications and services available from each genealogist.

APG
P.O. Box 40393
Denver, CO 80204-0393
URL:
http://www.apgen.org/~apg/
(Updated 1/31/98)
(Accessed 2/2/98)

Association of Professional Genealogists   The Association of Professional Genealogists (APG) was founded in 1979 to promote standards and ethics in the genealogical research and now claims over 1,000 members worldwide. Members include family historians, professional researchers, librarians, archivists, writers, editors, consultants, computer specialists, and many others.

The APG produces a quarterly journal for its members that covers issues such as professionalism, communication with clients, preparation of lineage society applications, training, research assistants, and preparation of manuscripts for printing.

APG publishes a biennial *Directory of Members* that is distributed worldwide to members, libraries, societies, and consumers. The directory includes members' biographies, services, research and geographic specialties. To order a copy of the latest *APG Directory of Professional Genealogists,* contact APG. Their order form is also on their Web site.

Family History Library   The Library offers accreditation in various geographical areas. Accredited Genealogists (AG) undergo a rigorous screening and testing process. They must renew their accreditation every five years. The accreditation test includes:

Handwriting: The ability to read a genealogical document (or documents).

Document recognition: Identification of important sources and reference works.

LDS Church records: Scholarship of the composition and application to research of records created by The Church of Jesus Christ of Latter-day Saints.

Brief pedigree evaluations: Provide a list of sources to be searched to extend each pedigree.

Pedigree problems: The examination gives an actual pedigree problem in which the researcher will carry out the research in the Family History Library and write a report.

General questions and answers: Knowledge of facts pertaining to the history and records of the chosen area.

Other Sources

Association of Professional Genealogists. *1997-98 APG Directory of Professional Genealogists.* Compiled and edited by Elizabeth Kelley Kerstens and Kathleen W. Hinckley. Denver: Association of Professional Genealogists, 1997. Available from: APG, PO Box 40393, Denver, CO 80204-0393.

Everton's Genealogical Helper Every year a "Directory of Professional Genealogical Researchers" is published in the September/October issue of *Everton's Genealogical Helper.* This directory places professional genealogical researchers under the subjects or geographical areas where they are qualified and willing to conduct research for others. They use a numbering system with a code. The list of numbers refers to the research categories where researchers are prepared to perform record searches. Readers may select a competent researcher from the directory.

Heritage Quest: The Genealogy Magazine Regular issues of this magazine list "Genealogists Who Will Do Research." The list is alphabetical by state with counties of specialty, followed by the name, address, telephone number, and email address. Researchers pay a fee to be listed in the directory.

The Internet Professional genealogists and their affiliations can be found on the Internet. Use one of the search engines and type in "+ genealogists +professional +(state)." You will get more names than you can use.

Summary

It is not unreasonable to hire someone to do genealogical research. In fact it could be the smartest, least expensive, and most efficient of all the options. Only the family historian can decide that. Librarians need to have information about hiring a professional to give their patrons access to this option.

Reasons to consider hiring a professional genealogist

- *The language the records are in is foreign to you.*

- *Political obstacles keep you from normal access to the records you need to search.*

- *Access to the records you need is limited by membership or credentials.*

- *You live a great distance from the records you need to search and you cannot afford to travel there in person.*

- *You lack the skills to search certain types or records.*

- *You are physically unable (including visual impairment) to do the research*

- *You want to verify what you have before you publish a book.*

- *You want to resolve any conflicts in the information you have.*

- *You are up against a short time frame and you needs some help completing your work before a deadline.*

- *You have searched every possible record you can think of and you don't know where else to turn.*

Chapter 10

Bringing It All Together

What you do with the product of genealogical research is an important topic. As a means of corroborating research that has been completed, and to add to the lines where dead ends seem to exist, every genealogist needs to publish or post what he or she as compiled. Who knows whether someone may see it and have data to add to what has already been done.

Publication can be as simple as photocopying a few copies of the completed work and giving it to family members and the library. It is also easy to put a genealogy on the Internet. Some sites might charge a fee, but when you consider the time and effort already invested by the researcher along with the possible new connections to be gained, this is well worth the expense.

The Family History Library is another possible way to share a genealogy. The Library will add a copy of any family genealogy sent to them as a GEDCOM file to the *Ancestral File*. Doing so doesn't mean the names will be submitted to a Mormon temple. Members of The Church of Jesus Christ of Latter-day Saints have to do that using a different process. They are instructed to submit only the names of people who are directly related to them, and that is all. The names they submit will eventually show up on the *International Genealogical Index*.

Sharing is the operative word in genealogical research. If genealogists were not willing to share the research they had compiled, everything might be lost. Several ways to share this research have been discussed, leaving the individual researcher to choose a method most appropriate for him or her.

Conclusion

This book was written to help librarians who provide reference service to genealogists. I wanted you to gain some insight into all the resources that are available to help your customer. I want you to be able to answer their questions with confidence. There is some excellent information in this book. I hope you can make good use of it. If you do, the genealogists you help will be very grateful for your outstanding service.

Even though this is a basic handbook, I have tried to provide you with enough detail so you wouldn't have to look up an address or a telephone number in another source.

I have also tried to give you a glimpse of all the resources that might contain the specific facts that all researchers seek. Now that you know more about places to look, you will be able to save some researchers time in their never-ending quest for their ancestors.

There was no way that I could include every library that provides service to genealogists; almost every library does. I selected a few that rose above the crowd— that seemed to do a more for genealogists.

If I were the librarian who had just finished reading this book I would ask myself "What can I do to use what I just learned from this book?" To help you answer this question I have created one last checklist on the next page.

Librarian's Action Checklist

✔ Review the library's materials selection policy, especially for genealogical and local history materials. Take recommended changes to the board.

✔ Review budget allocations for genealogical and local history materials.

✔ Review the recommended titles (for your size library) in this book and order the ones you don't have.

✔ Create a four-page handout for beginning genealogists that includes charts and information they need to get started.

✔ Find out where the nearest Family History Center is located.

✔ Go to your county courthouse and discover what they have that can help your patrons.

✔ Buy another copy of this book for the circulating collection.

✔ Create a handout that lists other facilities in the community that can provide information for genealogists.

✔ Buy one or more genealogy software programs and load them on a public access computer so your patrons can try them out.

✔ Buy some CD-ROMs with genealogical data on them and let the patrons use them.

✔ Use this book as a staff training manual.

✔ Start your own genealogy, if you aren't already into it up to your ears.

✔ Check out some of the URLs listed in this book.

✔ Create a notebook that lists major genealogical collections in your state or region.

✔ Contact at least one other librarian and ask him or her what they are doing to help genealogists.

The Last Word

When it comes to helping genealogist, be confident in your role as a librarian. You are good at what you do. You can answer the toughest questions in the world, with the right resources, or by referring the patron to another special library.

National Archives—Regional Archives System

National Archives—New England Region
380 Trapelo Rd.
Waltham, MA 02154
Tel: 617/647-8100
Area Served: Connecticut, Maine, Massachusetts, New Hampshire, Rhode Island, and Vermont

National Archives—Pittsfield Region
100 Dan Fox Dr.
Pittsfield, MA 01201
Tel: 413/445-6885
(No accessioned records, only microfilm relating to genealogy)

National Archives—Northeast Region
201 Varick St.
New York, NY 10014
Tel: 212/337-1300
Area Served: New Jersey, New York, Puerto Rico, and the Virgin Islands

National Archives—Mid Atlantic Region
Ninth and Market St., Rm. 1350
Philadelphia, PA 19107
Tel: 215/597-3000
Area Served: Delaware, Pennsylvania, Maryland, Virginia, and West Virginia

National Archives—Southeast Region
1557 St. Joseph Ave.
East Point, GA 30344
Tel: 404/763-7477
Area Served: Alabama, Florida, Georgia, Kentucky, Mississippi, North Carolina, South Carolina, and Tennessee

National Archives—Great Lakes Region
7358 South Pulaski Rd.
Chicago, IL 60629
Tel: 312/581-7816
Area Served: Illinois, Indiana, Michigan, Minnesota, Ohio, and Wisconsin

National Archives—Central Plains Region
2312 East Bannister Rd.
Kansas City, MO 64131
Tel: 816/926-6272
Area Served: Iowa, Kansas, Missouri, and Nebraska

National Archives—Southwest Region
501 West Felix St.
P.O. Box 6216
Fort Worth, TX 76115
Tel: 817/334-5525
Area Served: Arkansas, Louisiana, New Mexico, Oklahoma, and Texas

National Archives—Rocky Mountain Region
Building 48, Denver Federal Center
P.O. Box 25307
Denver, CO 80225
Tel: 303/236-0817
Area Served: Colorado, Montana, North Dakota, South Dakota, Utah, and Wyoming

National Archives—Pacific Southwest Region
24000 Avila Rd.
P.O. Box 6719
Laguna Niguel, CA 92607
Tel: 714/643-4241
Area Served: Arizona; southern California counties of Imperial, Inyo, Kern, Los Angeles, Orange, Riverside, San Bernardino, San Diego, San Luis Obispo, Santa Barbara, and Ventura; and Clark County, Nevada.

National Archives—Pacific Sierra Region
1000 Commodore Dr.
San Bruno, CA 94066
Tel: 415/876-9009
Area Served: North California, Hawaii, Nevada (except Clark County), American Samoa, and the Pacific Ocean area

National Archives—Pacific Northwest Region
6125 Sand Point Way, NE
Seattle, WA 98115
Tel: 206/526-6507
Area Served: Idaho, Oregon, and Washington

National Archives—Alaska Region
654 West Third Ave.
Anchorage, AK 99501
Tel: 907/271-2441
Area Served: Alaska

Publishers of Genealogical Materials

Scholarly Resources, Inc.
104 Greenhill Ave.
Wilmington, DE 19805-1897
Toll free: 800/772-8937
Email: scholres@ssnet.com

Genealogical Publishing Co., Inc.
1001 N. Calvert St.
Baltimore, MD 21202-3897
Toll free: 800/296-6687

Heritage Quest
P.O. Box 329
Bountiful, UT 84011-0329
Toll free: 800/298-5446
Fax: 801/298-5468

Everton Publishers, Inc.
P.O. Box 368
Logan, UT 84323-0368
Tel: 801/752-6022

Clearfield Company
200 East Eager St.
Baltimore, MD 21202
Tel: 410/625-9004

Family Historian Books
207 South 119th St.
Tacoma, WA 98444
Toll free: 800/535-0118

Heritage Books, Inc.
1540-E Pointer Ridge Pl.
Bowie, MD 20716
Toll free: 800/398-7709
Fax: 800/276-1760

Picton Press
P.O. Box 1111
Camden, ME 04843
Toll free: 800/742-8667
Fax: 207/236-6713

Frontier Press
P.O. Box 3715, Dept. 199
Galveston, TX 77552

Higginson Book Company
148-GH Washington St.
Salem, MA 01970

Resource Bibliography

This is a collected bibliography of resources described throughout the book.
For the complete annotation, see the page in the main text that is listed here.
For a list of genealogy software, see chapter 7, beginning on p. 93.
For a list of Web sites, see chapter 8, beginning on p. 97.

Allen, Desmond Walls, and Carolyn Earle Billingsley. *Beginner's Guide to Family History Research*. 3rd ed. Conway, Arkansas: Research Associates, 1997. ISBN: 1-56546-101-0: 45

American Genealogist (Box 398, Demorest, GA 30535-0398): 55

Ancestry Magazine (Ancestry Inc., PO Box 990, Orem, Utah 84059-0990): 53

Andriot, Jay, comp. *Township Atlas of the United States*. McLean, Virginia: Documents Index, 1991: 50

Askin, Jayne, and Molly Davis. *Search: A Handbook for Adoptees and Birthparents*. 2nd ed. Phoenix: Oryx, 1992. ISBN 0897747178: 24

Association of Professional Genealogists. *1997-98 APG Directory of Professional Genealogists*. Compiled and edited by Elizabeth Kelley Kerstens and Kathleen W. Hinckley. Denver: Association of Professional Genealogists, 1997: 109

Beller, Susan Provost. *Roots for Kids: A Genealogy Guide for Young People*. Baltimore: Genealogical Publishing, 1997. ISBN: 0-80631-525-3: 45

Bentley, Elizabeth Petty. *County Courthouse Book*. Baltimore: Genealogical Publishing, 1990. ISBN: 0-8063-1284-X: 49

————. *Directory of Family Associations*. 3rd ed. Baltimore: Genealogical Publishing, 1996. ISBN: 0-8063-1523-7: 49

————. *The Genealogist's Address Book*. 3rd ed. Baltimore: Genealogical Publishing, 1995. ISBN 0-8063-1455-9: 49

Billingsley, Carolyn E., and Desmond W. Allen. *How to Get the Most Out of Death Certificates*. Bryant, Arkansas: Research Associates, 1991: 24

Bonner, Laurie, and Steve Bonner. *Searching for Cyber-Roots: A Step-by-Step Guide to Genealogy on the World Wide Web*. Salt Lake City: Ancestry, 1997. ISBN: 0916489787: 106

Bremer, Ronald A. *Compendium of Historical Sources: The How and Where of American Genealogy*. Rev. ed., Bountiful, Utah: AGLL. 1997. ISBN: 1877677159: 47

Carlberg, Nancy Ellen. *Climbing the Family Tree with Nancy*. Anaheim, California: Carlberg Press, 1997. ISBN: 0-944878-00-8: 46

————. *How to Survive the Genealogy Bug Without Going Broke*. Anaheim, California: Carlberg Press, 1991. ISBN: 0-944878-22-9: 46

Cerny, Johni, and Wendy Elliot, eds. *The Library: A Guide to the LDS Family History Library*. Salt Lake City: Ancestry, 1988. ISBN: 0-916489-21-3: 59

Connecticut Nutmegger (Connecticut Society of Genealogists, PO Box 435, Glastonbury, CT 06033): 55

Cooper, Brian, ed. *The Internet*. New York: DK Publishing, 1996. ISBN: 0789412888: 106

Cosgriff, John and Carolyn. *Turbo Genealogy: An Introduction to Family History Research in the Information Age*. Salt Lake City: Ancestry, 1997: 105

Crandall, Ralph J. *Shaking Your Family Tree: A Basic Guide to Tracing Your Family's Genealogy*. Camden, Maine: Yankee Books, 1988. ISBN: 0-89909-148-2: 46

Croom, Emily Anne. *The Genealogist's Companion & Sourcebook*. Cincinnati: Betterway Books, 1994. ISBN 1-55870-331-4: 46

————. *Unpuzzling Your Past: A Basic Guide to Genealogy*. 3rd ed. Cincinnati: Betterway Books, 1995. ISBN: 1-55870-396-9: 46

————. *Unpuzzling Your Past Workbook: Essential Forms and Letters for All Genealogists*. Cincinnati: Betterway Books, 1996. ISBN: 155870423X: 46

Crowe, Elizabeth Powell. *Genealogy Online: Researching Your Roots*. 2nd ed. New York: McGraw-Hill, 1996. ISBN 0-07-014754-X: 105

Davenport, Robert R. *Hereditary Society Blue Book*. Baltimore: Genealogical Publishing, 1994. ISBN: 0-8063-1398-6: 47

DeBartolo, Sharon. *A Genealogist's Guide to Discovering Your Female Ancestors: Special Strategies for Uncovering Hard-to-Find Information about Your Female Lineage*. Cincinnati: Betterway Books, 1998. ISBN 1-55870-472-8: 48

Directory of Deceased American Physicians 1804-1929. 2 vols. Arthur W. Hafner, Ph.D., ed. Chicago: American Medical Association, 1993. ISBN: 0-89970-527-8: 49

Directory of Historical Organizations in the United States and Canada. 14th ed. Edited by Mary Bray Wheeler. Nashville: American Association for State and Local History, 1990. ISBN: 0-942063-05-8: 50

Dollarhide, William. *Genealogy Starter Kit*. Baltimore: Genealogical Publishing, 1994. ISBN: 0-8063-1410-9: 46

Donald Lines Jacobus' Index to Genealogical Periodicals. 3rd. ed. Revised by Carl Boyer. Camden, Maine: Picton Press, 1995. ISBN: 0-897252-38-1: 53

Eichholz, Alice, ed. *Ancestry's Red Book: American State, County & Town Sources*. Salt Lake City: Ancestry, 1992. ISBN 0-916489-47-7: 30

Everton's Genealogical Helper (PO Box 368, Logan, Utah 84321): 53

Family History SourceGuide, (CD-ROM) Salt Lake City: The Church of Jesus Christ of Latter-day Saints, 1998: 45

FGS Forum (Federation of Genealogical Societies, PO Box 3385, Salt Lake City, UT 84110): 53

Filby, P. William. *A Bibliography of American County Histories*. Baltimore: Genealogical Publishing, 1985. ISBN 0-8063-1126-6: 51

Flores, Norma P., and Patsy Ludwig. *A Beginner's Guide to Hispanic Genealogy (Introducción a la Investigación Genealógical Latino Americana)*. San Mateo, Calif.: Western Press, 1993. ISBN: 0-936029-31-5: 47

Genealogical Computing (Ancestry Inc., PO Box 476, Salt Lake City, UT 84110-0476): 53

Genealogical Journal (PO Box 1144, Salt Lake City, UT 84110): 54

Genealogy Bulletin (American Genealogical Lending Library, PO Box 329, Bountiful, UT 84011-0329): 54

Greene, Evarts B., and Virginia D. Harrington. *American Population Before the Federal Census of 1790*. Baltimore: Genealogical Publishing. Reprint 1993: 61

Greenwood, Val D. *The Researcher's Guide to American Genealogy*. 2d ed. Baltimore: Genealogical Publishing, 1990. ISBN: 0-8063-1267-X: 45

Grundset, Eric G., and Steven B. Rhodes. *American Genealogical Research at the DAR*. Washington DC: National Society, DAR, 1997. ISBN 0-9602528-9-4: 48

Handy Book for Genealogists: United States of America. 8th ed. Logan, Utah: Everton Publishers, 1998. ISBN 1-890895-03-2: 45

Helmbold, F. Wilbur. *Tracing Your Ancestry: A Step-by-Step Guide to Researching Your Family History*. Birmingham: Oxmoor, 1985. ISBN: 0-8487-0486-X: 47

Heritage Quest Magazine (PO Box 329, Bountiful, UT 84011-0329): 54

Hone, E. Wade. *Land and Property Research in the United States*. Salt Lake City: Ancestry, 1997. ISBN: 0-916489-68-X: 48

Hoosier Genealogist (Indiana Historical Society, 315 W. Ohio Street, Indianapolis, IN 46202-3299): 55

Illinois State Genealogical Society Quarterly (Illinois State Genealogical Society, PO Box 10195, Springfield, IL 62791): 55

Johnson, Richard S. *How to Locate Anyone Who Is or Has Been in the Military, Armed Forces Locator Directory*. Ft. Sam Houston, TX: Military Information Enterprises, 1990. ISBN 1-877639-01-X: 50

Kaminkow, Marion J., ed. *A Complement to Genealogies in the Library of Congress: A Bibliography*. Baltimore: Magna Carta Book, 1981. ISBN: 0-910946-25-6: 51

————. *U.S. Local Histories in the Library of Congress: A Bibliography*. 5 vols. Baltimore: Magna Carta Book, 1975-76. ISBN 0-910946-17-5: 51

Howells, Cyndi. *Netting Your Ancestors: Genealogical Research on the Internet*. Baltimore: Genealogical Publishing, 1997. ISBN: 0-8063-1546-6: 104

Kansas Atlas and Gazetteer: Topographic Maps of the Entire State. Freeport, Maine: DeLorme, 1997. ISBN: 0-89933-215-3: 51

Kemp, Thomas Jay, *The 1995 Genealogy Annual: A Bibliography of Published Sources*. Wilmington, Delaware: Scholarly Resources, 1996. ISBN: 0-8420-2661-4: 51

————. *Virtual Roots: A Guide to Genealogy and Local History on the World Wide Web*. Wilmington, Delaware: Scholarly Resources, 1997. ISBN: 0-8420-2718-1 (cloth), ISBN 0-8420-2720-3 (paper): 105

Kentucky Ancestors (Kentucky Historical Society, Old State Capitol, PO Box 1792, Frankfort, KY 40602-1792): 55

Konrad, J. *Directory of Family "One-Name" Periodicals*. Munroe Falls, Ohio: Summit: 53

Kot, Elizabeth G., and James D. Kot. *United States Cemetery Address Book*. Vallejo, California: Indices Publishing, 1995. ISBN: 0-9641213-2-8: 50

Life Story: The Family and Community Writer's Workshop (3591 Letter Rock Rd., Manhattan, KS 66502): 54

Magazine of Virginia Genealogy (Virginia Genealogical Society, 5001 W. Broad St., Ste. 115, Richmond, VA 23230-3023): 55

Mayflower Quarterly, A Journal of Family History in Colonial New England (General Society of Mayflower Descendants, PO Box 3297, Plymouth, MA 02361): 54

Mills, Elizabeth Shown. *Evidence! Citation and Analysis for the Family Historian*. Baltimore: Genealogical Publishing, 1997. ISBN 0-8063-1543-1: 39

National Archives Microfilm Resources for Research: A Comprehensive Catalog. Washington, DC: National Archives Trust Fund Board, 1987. ISBN 0-911333-34-7: 30

National Genealogical Newsletter (PO Box 870212, University of Alabama, Tuscaloosa, AL 35487-0212): 62

National Genealogical Society Quarterly (PO Box 870212, University of Alabama, Tuscaloosa, AL 35487-0212): 62

Neagles, James C. *The Library of Congress: A Guide to Genealogical and Historical Research*. Salt Lake City, Utah: Ancestry, 1990. ISBN: 0-916489-484: 64

New England Historic Genealogical Society. *Circulating Library. Circulating Library Catalog for the New England Historic Genealogical Society*. 2 vols. 7th ed. Boston: New England Historic Genealogical Society, 1996: 51

New England Historical and Genealogical Register (101 Newbury St., Boston, MA 02116): 54

New York Genealogical and Biographical Record (122 E. 58th St., New York, NY 10022): 54

Newberry Library, Chicago. *The Genealogical Index*. Boston: G.K. Hall, 1960. Microfilm. ISBN 0-8161-1317-3. 8 reels: 51

North Carolina Genealogical Society Journal (Box 1492, Raleigh NC 27602): 55

Oldfield, Jim. *Your Family Tree Using Your PC*. Grand Rapids, MI: Abacus, 1997. ISBN: 1-55755-310-6: 106

Parker, J. Carlyle. *Going to Salt Lake City to Do Family History Research*. 3rd ed. Turlock, California: Marrietta Publishing, 1996. ISBN: 0-934153-14-0:   59

PERSI: Periodical Source Index CD-ROM for Windows, Orem, Utah: Ancestry, 1997:   52

Przecha, Donna, and Joan Lowrey. *Guide to Genealogy Software*. Baltimore: Genealogical Publishing, 1993. ISBN 080631382X: 93

Prologue: The Quarterly of the National Archives (NEPS-Rm. G-6, National Archives, Washington, D.C. 20408):   54

Rand, McNally. *Commercial Atlas and Marketing Guide*. Chicago:Rand McNally 1997:   51

Reamy, Martha, and William Reamy, comp. *Index to the Roll of Honor (Civil War)*. Baltimore: Genealogical Publishing, 1995. ISBN: 0-8063-1483-4:   50

Rillera, Mary Jo. *The Adoption Searchbook: Techniques for Tracing People*. 3d rev. ed. Westminster, California: Pure Inc., 1991. ISBN: 0910143005:   24

Schaefer, Christina K. *The Center: A Guide to Genealogical Research in the National Capital Area*. Baltimore: Genealogical Publishing, 1996. ISBN: 0-8063-1515-6: 48

———. *Guide to Naturalization Records of The United States*. Baltimore: Genealogical Publishing, 1997. ISBN: 0-8063-1532-6:   48

Second Boat (Pentref Press, PO Box 2782, Kennebunkport, ME 04046-2782):   55

Southern Queries (PO Box 23854, Columbia, SC 29224-3854):   55

Stryker-Rodda, Harriet. *How to Climb Your Family Tree: Genealogy for Beginners*. Baltimore: Genealogical Publishing, 1993. ISBN 0-8161-5021-4:   47

———. *Understanding Colonial Handwriting*. Baltimore: Genealogical Publishing, 1996. ISBN: 0-80631-525-3:   47

Szucs, Loretto Dennis, and Sandra Hargreaves Luebking. *The Archives: A Guide to The National Archives Field Branches*. Salt Lake City: Ancestry, 1988. ISBN: 0-916489-23-X: 48

———. *The Source: A Guidebook of American Genealogy*. Salt Lake City: Ancestry, 1997. ISBN: 0-916489-67-1: 30

Tepper, Michael. *American Passenger Arrival Records. A Guide to the Records of Immigrants Arriving at American Ports by Sail and Steam*. Baltimore: Genealogical Publishing, 1996. ISBN: 0-8063-1380-3:   48

Thorndale, William, and William Dollarhide. *Map Guide to the U.S. Federal Censuses 1790-1920*. Baltimore: Genealogical Publishing, 1995. ISBN: 0806311886:   49

U.S. Library of Congress. *Genealogies Cataloged by the Library of Congress Since 1986: With a List of Established Forms of Family Names and a List of Genealogies Converted to Microfilm Since 1983*. Washington, D.C.: Library of Congress, 1992:   52

United States Local Histories in the Library of Congress: A Bibliography. Marion J. Kaminkow, ed. Baltimore: Genealogical Publishing, 1976. ISBN: 0-614-10566-8: 52

United States. National Archives and Records Administration. *Guide to Federal Records in the National Archives of the United States*. Washington, DC: National Archives and Records Administration: 61

U.S. National Center for Health Statistics. *Where to Write for Vital Records: Births. Deaths, Marriages, and Divorces*. DHHS Pub. No. (PHS) 93-1142. Hyattsville, MD: National Center for Health Statistics, 1993. ISBN 0-160362-75-X: 47

University Microfilms International. *Family Histories for Genealogists: A Microfiche Program from UMI*. Ann Arbor: University Microfilms International, 1987:   52

Whitaker, Beverly DeLong. *Beyond Pedigrees: Organizing and Enhancing Your Work*. Salt Lake City: Ancestry, 1993. ISBN: 0-916489-52-3:   47

Index